John Wesley Powell
and the Great Surveys of the American West

General Editor

William H. Goetzmann
Jack S. Blanton, Sr., Chair in History
  University of Texas at Austin

Consulting Editor

Tom D. Crouch
Chairman, Department of Aeronautics
  National Air and Space Museum
  Smithsonian Institution

WORLD EXPLORERS

John Wesley Powell
and the Great Surveys of the American West

Ann Gaines

Introductory Essay by Michael Collins

CHELSEA HOUSE PUBLISHERS

New York · Philadelphia

On the cover Gorlinski's 1868 Land Office map of the western United States; portrait of John Wesley Powell

Chelsea House Publishers
Editor-in-Chief Remmel Nunn
Managing Editor Karyn Gullen Browne
Copy Chief Mark Rifkin
Picture Editor Adrian G. Allen
Art Director Maria Epes
Assistant Art Director Howard Brotman
Series Design Loraine Machlin
Manufacturing Director Gerald Levine
Systems Manager Lindsey Ottman
Production Manager Joseph Romano
Production Coordinator Marie Claire Cebrián

World Explorers
Senior Editor Sean Dolan

Staff for JOHN WESLEY POWELL AND THE GREAT SURVEYS
OF THE AMERICAN WEST
Copy Editor Christopher Duffy
Assistant Editor Martin Mooney
Picture Researcher Diana Gongora
Senior Designer Basia Niemczyc

3 5 7 9 8 6 4 2

Library of Congress Cataloging-in-Publication Data

Gaines, Ann.
John Wesley Powell and the great surveys of the American West/ Ann Gaines.
p.   cm.—(World explorers)
Includes bibliographical references and index.
Summary: A biography of the geologist who first explored the Colorado River and the Grand Canyon.
ISBN 0-7910-1318-9
        0-7910-1542-4 (pbk.)
1. Powell, John Wesley, 1834–1902—Juvenile literature.
2. Explorers—United States—Biography—Juvenile literature.
3. Colorado River (Colo.–Mexico)—Discovery and exploration—Juvenile literature.   4. Grand Canyon (Ariz.)—Discovery and exploration—Juvenile literature.   5. United States—Exploring expeditions—Juvenile literature.   [1. Powell, John Wesley, 1834–1902.   2. Explorers.   3. Geologists.   4. Colorado River (Colo.–Mexico)—Discovery and exploration.   5. Grand Canyon (Ariz.)—Discovery and exploration.   6. United States—Exploring expeditions.]   I. Title.   II. Series.
                                                        91-28329
F788.P93G35   1992   CIP
979.1'3—dc20   AC

CONTENTS

WORLD EXPLORERS

THE EARLY EXPLORERS

Herodotus and the Explorers of the Classical Age
Marco Polo and the Medieval Explorers
The Viking Explorers

THE FIRST GREAT AGE OF DISCOVERY

Jacques Cartier, Samuel de Champlain, and the Explorers of Canada
Christopher Columbus and the First Voyages to the New World
From Coronado to Escalante: The Explorers of the Spanish Southwest
Hernando de Soto and the Explorers of the American South
Sir Francis Drake and the Struggle for an Ocean Empire
Vasco da Gama and the Portuguese Explorers
La Salle and the Explorers of the Mississippi
Ferdinand Magellan and the Discovery of the World Ocean
Pizarro, Orellana, and the Exploration of the Amazon
The Search for the Northwest Passage
Giovanni da Verrazano and the Explorers of the Atlantic Coast

THE SECOND GREAT AGE OF DISCOVERY

Roald Amundsen and the Quest for the South Pole
Daniel Boone and the Opening of the Ohio Country
Captain James Cook and the Explorers of the Pacific
The Explorers of Alaska
John Charles Frémont and the Great Western Reconnaissance
Alexander von Humboldt, Colossus of Exploration
Lewis and Clark and the Route to the Pacific
Alexander Mackenzie and the Explorers of Canada
Robert Peary and the Quest for the North Pole
Zebulon Pike and the Explorers of the American Southwest
John Wesley Powell and the Great Surveys of the American West
Jedediah Smith and the Mountain Men of the American West
Henry Stanley and the European Explorers of Africa
Lt. Charles Wilkes and the Great U.S. Exploring Expedition

THE THIRD GREAT AGE OF DISCOVERY

Apollo to the Moon
The Explorers of the Undersea World
The First Men in Space
The Mission to Mars and Beyond
Probing Deep Space

CHELSEA HOUSE PUBLISHERS

Into the Unknown

Michael Collins

It is difficult to define most eras in history with any precision, but not so the space age. On October 4, 1957, it burst on us with little warning when the Soviet Union launched *Sputnik*, a 184-pound cannonball that circled the globe once every 96 minutes. Less than 4 years later, the Soviets followed this first primitive satellite with the flight of Yury Gagarin, a 27-year-old fighter pilot who became the first human to orbit the earth. The Soviet Union's success prompted President John F. Kennedy to decide that the United States should "land a man on the moon and return him safely to earth" before the end of the 1960s. We now had not only a space age but a space race.

I was born in 1930, exactly the right time to allow me to participate in Project Apollo, as the U.S. lunar program came to be known. As a young man growing up, I often found myself too young to do the things I wanted—or suddenly too old, as if someone had turned a switch at midnight. But for Apollo, 1930 was the perfect year to be born, and I was very lucky. In 1966 I enjoyed circling the earth for three days, and in 1969 I flew to the moon and laughed at the sight of the tiny earth, which I could cover with my thumbnail.

How the early explorers would have loved the view from space! With one glance Christopher Columbus could have plotted his course and reassured his crew that the world was indeed round. In 90 minutes Magellan could have looked down at every port of call in the *Victoria*'s three-year circumnavigation of the globe. Given a chance to map their route from orbit, Lewis and Clark could have told President Jefferson that there was no easy Northwest Passage but that a continent of exquisite diversity awaited their scrutiny.

In a physical sense, we have already gone to most places that we can. That is not to say that there are not new adventures awaiting us deep in the sea or on the red plains of Mars, but more important than reaching new places will be understanding those we have already visited. There are vital gaps in our understanding of how our planet works as an ecosystem and how our planet fits into the infinite order of the universe. The next great age may well be the age of assimilation, in which we use microscope and telescope to evaluate what we have discovered and put that knowledge to use. The adventure of being first to reach may be replaced by the satisfaction of being first to grasp. Surely that is a form of exploration as vital to our well-being, and perhaps even survival, as the distinction of being the first to explore a specific geographical area.

The explorers whose stories are told in the books of this series did not just sail perilous seas, scale rugged mountains, traverse blistering deserts, dive to the depths of the ocean, or land on the moon. Their voyages and expeditions were journeys of mind as much as of time and distance, through which they—and all of mankind—were able to reach a greater understanding of our universe. That challenge remains, for all of us. The imperative is to see, to understand, to develop knowledge that others can use, to help nurture this planet that sustains us all. Perhaps being born in 1975 will be as lucky for a new generation of explorer as being born in 1930 was for Neil Armstrong, Buzz Aldrin, and Mike Collins.

The Reader's Journey

William H. Goetzmann

This volume is one of a series that takes us with the great explorers of the ages on bold journeys over the oceans and the continents and into outer space. As we travel along with these imaginative and courageous journeyers, we share their adventures and their knowledge. We also get a glimpse of that mysterious and inextinguishable fire that burned in the breast of men such as Magellan and Columbus—the fire that has propelled all those throughout the ages who have been driven to leave behind family and friends for a voyage into the unknown.

No one has ever satisfactorily explained the urge to explore, the drive to go to the "back of beyond." It is certain that it has been present in man almost since he began walking erect and first ventured across the African savannas. Sparks from that same fire fueled the transoceanic explorers of the Ice Age, who led their people across the vast plain that formed a land bridge between Asia and North America, and the astronauts and scientists who determined that man must reach the moon.

Besides an element of adventure, all exploration involves an element of mystery. We must not confuse exploration with discovery. Exploration is a purposeful human activity—a search for something. Discovery may be the end result of that search; it may also be an accident, as when Columbus found a whole new world while searching for the Indies. Often, the explorer may not even realize the full significance of what he has discovered, as was the case with Columbus. Exploration, on the other hand, is the product of a cultural or individual curiosity; it is a unique process that has enabled mankind to know and understand the world's oceans, continents, and polar regions. It is at the heart of scientific thinking. One of its most significant aspects is that it teaches people to ask the right questions; by doing so, it forces us to reevaluate what we think we know and understand. Thus knowledge progresses, and we are driven constantly to a new awareness and appreciation of the universe in all its infinite variety.

The motivation for exploration is not always pure. In his fascination with the new, man often forgets that others have been there before him. For example, the popular notion of the discovery of America overlooks the complex Indian civilizations that had existed there for thousands of years before the arrival of Europeans. Man's desire for conquest, riches, and fame is often linked inextricably with his quest for the unknown, but a story that touches so closely on the human essence must of necessity treat war as well as peace, avarice with generosity, both pride and humility, frailty and greatness. The story of exploration is above all a story of humanity and of man's understanding of his place in the universe.

The WORLD EXPLORERS series has been divided into four sections. The first treats the explorers of the ancient world, the Viking explorers of the 9th through the 11th centuries, and Marco Polo and the medieval explorers. The rest of the series is divided into three great ages of exploration. The first is the era of Columbus and Magellan: the period spanning the 15th and 16th centuries, which saw the discovery and exploration of the New World and the world ocean. The second might be called the age of science and imperialism, the era made possible by the scientific advances of the 17th century, which witnessed the discovery of the world's last two undiscovered continents, Australia and Antarctica, the mapping of all the continents and oceans, and the establishment of colonies all over the world. The third great age refers to the most ambitious quests of the 20th century—the probing of space and of the ocean's depths.

As we reach out into the darkness of outer space and other galaxies, we come to better understand how our ancestors confronted *oecumene*, or the vast earthly unknown. We learn once again the meaning of an unknown 18th-century sea captain's advice to navigators:

> And if by chance you make a landfall on the shores of another sea in a far country inhabited by savages and barbarians, remember you this: the greatest danger and the surest hope lies not with fires and arrows but in the quicksilver hearts of men.

At its core, exploration is a series of moral dramas. But it is these dramas, involving new lands, new people, and exotic ecosystems of staggering beauty, that make the explorers' stories not only moral tales but also some of the greatest adventure stories ever recorded. They represent the process of learning in its most expansive and vivid forms. We see that real life, past and present, transcends even the adventures of the starship *Enterprise*.

1869. May 10th. 1869.

GREAT EVENT

Rail Road from the Atlantic to the Pacific

GRAND OPENING

OF THE

Union Pacific

RAIL ROAD,

PLATTE VALLEY ROUTE.

PASSENGER TRAINS LEAVE

OMAHA

ON THE ARRIVAL OF TRAINS FROM THE EAST.

THROUGH TO SAN FRANCISCO

In less than Four Days, avoiding the Dangers of the Sea!

Travelers for Pleasure, Health or Business

Will find a Trip over The Rocky Mountains Healthy and Pleasant.

LUXURIOUS CARS & EATING HOUSES

ON THE UNION PACIFIC RAIL ROAD.

PULLMAN'S PALACE SLEEPING CARS

RUN WITH ALL THROUGH PASSENGER TRAINS.

GOLD, SILVER AND OTHER MINERS!

Now is the time to seek your Fortunes in Nebraska, Wyoming, Arizona, Washington, Dakotah Colorado, Utah, Oregon, Montana, New Mexico, Idaho, Nevada or California.

CONNECTIONS MADE AT

CHEYENNE for DENVER, CENTRAL CITY & SANTA FE

AT OGDEN AND CORINNE FOR HELENA, BOISE CITY, VIRGINIA CITY, SALT LAKE CITY AND ARIZONA.

THROUGH TICKETS FOR SALE AT ALL PRINCIPAL RAILROAD OFFICES!

Be Sure they Read via Platte Valley or Omaha

Company's Office 72 La Salle St., opposite City Hall and Court House Square, Chicago.

CHARLES E. NICHOLS, Ticket Agent.

G. P. GILMAN,	JOHN P. HART,	J. BUDD,	W. SNYDER,
Gen'l Pass. Agt. 72 La Salle St., Chicago.	Gen'l Ticket Agt., Omaha, Neb.	Gen'l Ticket Agt., Omaha, Neb.	Gen'l Superintendent, Omaha, Neb.

Settled but Not Explored

When shabby, bluecoated General Ulysses S. Grant accepted the surrender of the Confederate forces from immaculately polished General Robert E. Lee at the small Virginia crossroads of Appomattox Courthouse on the morning of April 9, 1865, it marked the end of four years of the most brutal warfare imaginable. The Civil War—the inevitable and tragic culmination of several decades of bitter sectional conflict over the question of slavery—had divided the United States, for all intents and purposes, into two separate nations, North and South, and tested the limits, resiliency, and power of the Constitution as no crisis before or since. When the war finally ended on that fateful April day, the South lay defeated, prostrate, and in ruins, its economy demolished, an entire generation of its young men wounded, killed, or scarred in battle, its towns and countryside ravaged, and its most dominant and characteristic cultural and economic institution—slavery—forever abolished.

The North had also suffered greatly. Although the great majority of the fighting, and therefore the resulting destruction of property, occurred in the South, hundreds of thousands of men from the Northern states were also killed or wounded in the course of the bloody conflict. But for the North at least, this blood sacrifice had not been in vain, for its victory ensured that its interpretation of the

The completion of the transcontinental railroad in May 1869 was perhaps the single greatest spur to the settlement of the American West. As the railroad poster seen here indicates, it made it possible for passengers to travel from Omaha, Nebraska, "through to San Francisco In less than Four Days, avoiding the Dangers of the Sea." The poster also advised "Gold, Silver, and other miners" that "Now is the time to seek your Fortunes in Nebraska, Wyoming, Arizona, Washington, Dakotah[,] Colorado, Utah, Oregon, Montana, New Mexico, Idaho, Nevada or California."

Constitution, its view of the proper extent of the powers of the federal government, and its pattern of economic development would prevail. At its most basic, this meant that the union of the individual states could not be dissolved, that the federal government constitutionally possessed several fundamental powers that superseded those of the states, and that industrial, not agrarian, forms of economic development would prevail in the decades to come. As manifested in the states' disagreement over slavery, these issues had divided the country and threatened the union virtually from its inception.

Perhaps no event in American history has been as monumental as the Civil War. Its effects were numerous and extended to virtually every aspect of American society; entire lifetimes and whole sections of libraries have been devoted to their analysis. For obvious reasons, the war is usually regarded as a sectional conflict, pitting the two halves of the nation against each other for the sake of their differing and ultimately irreconcilable visions of the true meaning of the Constitution.

Yet in attempting to understand this period, the student of American history should remember that there is a third section to be considered, one larger in territory than the North and South combined. Although the Civil War was largely fought east of the Mississippi River—there were some exceptions to this generalization, especially in Missouri—it and the conflicts that created it were crucial in determining the course of the West's development. Until the Civil War, virtually every question pertaining to the West's use and settlement—at least in the chambers of Congress, the halls of the White House, and the rooms where the cabinet met—became inextricably entangled with the issues that split North and South. Indeed, in the years leading to the War Between the States, disagreements pertaining to the disposition of the western lands ignited the most heated controversies concerning the North and the South.

The most persistent of these controversies concerned the issue of statehood. How, or whether, the sprawling expanses west of the Mississippi were to be organized into legal entities and admitted to the Union with full privileges as states was of paramount importance to the existing states. By virtue of a tacit political agreement reached at the Constitutional Convention of 1787, for much of the 19th century Congress strove to maintain a rough political balance between North and South. Basically, this was achieved by a congressional policy of admitting slaveholding and free states on an alternate basis, so that a numerical balance between the two was maintained. For example, when Alabama was admitted to the Union in 1819, it became the 11th slaveholding state; at the time there were 11 free states in the North.

That same year, Missouri applied to Congress for statehood, with a proposed state constitution that allowed slavery. Missouri was only the second territory west of the Mississippi to apply for statehood, but it was the first region whose admission would constitute an extension of slavery into new territory. As Missouri's statehood threatened to demolish the existing balance of power, the prospect of its admission provoked an unprecedented crisis. Under the French and the Spanish, its previous owners, Louisiana, which was the first trans-Mississippi state to apply for and attain statehood, had always practiced slavery, a tradition Congress did not attempt to tamper with. Similarly, slavery had always been practiced in Alabama and had never been legal in the northern territory of Illinois, which was admitted as a free state in 1818.

But both North and South regarded Missouri's application as critical because it threatened to set a precedent for the subsequent treatment of the entire West as it became eligible for statehood. Northerners opposed to slavery regarded its successful confinement to the already existing southern states as the necessary first step to its complete eradication, while southerners believed its extension into the western territories to be absolutely crucial to the South's economic development and political well-being. Both regions feared that the other, by encouraging the development of either slave or free economies in the West and then stage-managing the admission of selected regions as states, could emerge with more votes for its interests in Congress. Political leaders from both the North and the South threatened that their states would seccdc, or leave the Union, if—depending on their state of origin—Missouri was or was not admitted.

Ultimately, as regarded Missouri, a compromise was reached. Missouri was admitted as a slave state and Maine—previously part of Massachusetts—was admitted as a free state, thus maintaining the balance of free and slave states in Congress. For the future, slavery was to be prohibited within the territory of the Louisiana Purchase north of latitude 36 degrees 30 minutes and allowed below that parallel. (The Louisiana Purchase was an immense tract of land that President Thomas Jefferson had purchased from France in 1803; it stretched from the Mississippi River to the Rocky Mountains and from the Gulf of Mexico to roughly the present-day border of the United States and Canada.)

The Missouri Compromise averted catastrophe for a time, but the most prescient minds of the young republic recognized that the respite was only temporary. Former president Thomas Jefferson wrote of the issue of the extension of slavery to the West that "this momentous question, like a fire bell in the night, awakened and filled me with terror. I considered it at once as the knell of the Union." John Adams, his fellow Founding Father, onetime political rival, and predecessor as president, was similarly concerned. "I take it for granted that the present question is a mere preamble—a title page to a great tragic volume," he wrote.

Because American settlement of that portion of the continent that would become the United States proceeded from the eastern seaboard westward, the western frontier had always been the subject of hopes, dreams, and aspirations denied or unavailable in the East. It has been for countless emigrants the land of opportunity within the Land of Opportunity. But this has meant as well that the West has often been a place where conceptions rooted in eastern experience, not the very different reality of the western environment, have held sway. More than one pioneer was overwhelmed by the contrast between his expectations and what he actually found in the West. The mythology spoke of virgin lands beckoning to the settler and pioneer; the reality was that the lands were in no way "virgin" and had been inhabited by hundreds of Indian nations for thousands of years. The mythology spoke of thousands of acres of fertile homesteads; the reality, in many cases, was treeless plains across which winds howled many months out of the year, carrying off the topsoil, where water was scarce and wood virtually nonexistent. All too often, the mythology ignored the reality that conflicts unresolved in the East were destined to be played out across the Mississippi.

Thus, although little in the climate and topography of the majority of the West suggested that it would be well suited for an economy based on slave labor, many southerners continued to envision it as fertile ground for slavery's expansion. Southerners were among the most fervent supporters of the Mexican War (1846–48), which they viewed as an opportunity to add new territory to the United States—territory into which slavery could presumably be introduced. By virtue of the war with Mexico, the United States gained the territory that would become the future states of New Mexico, Arizona, California, Nevada, Utah, and Colorado—the American Southwest. Many southerners were ecstatic about the acquisition—many northerners were pleased, too, but for different reasons— but when California in 1850 petitioned to enter the Union as a free state, another crisis arose. Already threatened by the proposed Wilmot Proviso, which would have prohibited slavery in any of the territory acquired from Mexico, the southern states again threatened secession. Only a series of compromises, engineered in the Senate by Henry Clay of Kentucky and Stephen Douglas of Illinois, preserved the Union and secured California's admission.

The Great Compromise, as the arrangement came to be known, did not nullify the Missouri Compromise, which applied only to Louisiana Purchase territory, but the proposal, in 1854, that the territories of Kansas and Nebraska be organized as states along the principal of "popular sovereignty," that is, by allowing their inhabitants to decide on the question of slavery, reignited the debate. As both territories were above latitude 36 degrees 30 minutes, the parallel north of which, according to the Missouri Compromise, slavery was to be forbidden "forever," northerners were incensed by the proposal. Both slavery supporters and abolitionists flocked to Kansas to influence the voting there, and the bloodshed that ensued earned it the sobriquet Bleeding Kansas.

By the time the Civil War began in 1861, the territory of the United States had reached, with the exception of Alaska, its current continental extent. It stretched from the Atlantic Ocean to the Pacific, from the Gulf of Mexico to the 49th parallel, but one-third of this area, all of it west of the Mississippi, had not yet been organized into states. Between Minnesota and Oregon and between Texas and the Canadian border, there were no states. In part, this was because of the constitutional crises that were created seemingly each time a western territory applied for statehood, and in larger part because so much of the vast western lands remained only sparsely settled. But this last cause was in itself to a great extent the effect of the tremendous conflict that rent the nation, for the project that would prove to be the single greatest stimulus to the settlement of the West—the construction of the transcontinental railroad—had fallen hostage to sectional politics.

Ulysses S. Grant was commander in chief of the Union forces during much of the Civil War; his relentlessness ultimately broke the South's will to resist. Most of the important work of the four great surveys of the American West was carried out during Grant's two terms as president.

In 1853, Congress had authorized the Secretary of War, Jefferson Davis (who just eight years later would become president of the Confederacy), to conduct a survey to determine the "most practicable and economical" route for a transcontinental railroad. Making use of the Army Corps of Topographical Engineers, an elite, highly trained cadre of West Point officers that between the Mexican and Civil wars conducted more than two dozen surveys of the West, Davis sent five separate survey teams into the field in 1853 and 1854 to test the feasibility of four proposed routes, each of which had powerful proponents.

Isaac Stevens, who had recently resigned his army commission to become governor of the Washington Territory, was given command of the northernmost survey, which was to explore a proposed route between the 47th and 49th parallels from the Great Lakes westward along the upper Missouri River and all the way to Puget Sound. Stevens was a protégé of the powerful Illinois senator Stephen Douglas, who strongly supported this route. Stevens was aided in his labors by Captain George B. McClellan, who would go on to command the Union forces in the Civil War and wage an unsuccessful campaign for president in 1864.

The 38th parallel route had long been championed by Senator Thomas Hart Benton, who, despite his opposition to the extension of slavery, had been Missouri's senator since it became a state. One of the most influential men in Congress and a staunch advocate of western expansion, Benton had lobbied long and hard to secure the command of this survey for his son-in-law, John Frémont, who had won fame as "the Pathfinder" for three previous exploratory reconnaissances of the West, often guided by the legendary scout Kit Carson. Frémont's reputation had been tarnished somewhat, however, by his court-martial for supposedly insubordinate actions during the Bear Flag rebellion (as the uprising of American settlers in California against Mexican rule there was known) and the Mexican War, and he had resigned his commission. Furthermore, Davis, a Mississippian, did not appreciate his or Benton's antislavery views. Command of the survey went instead to John W. Gunnison, who at age 41 was one of the topographical corps' most able and experienced officers. Although there is little doubt about Gunnison's qualifications for the position, he apparently had his doubts about the practicality of the suggested route, which would wend below the Uinta Mountains and the Great Salt Lake, and there is evidence to suggest, as the historian of exploration William H. Goetzmann has written, "that Davis sent the party into the field with the object of proving Benton wrong, rather than locating a railroad route."

The third proposed route, along roughly the 35th parallel, was backed by Representative John Smith Phelps of Missouri and the citizens of Arkansas, Tennessee, and Mississippi, as it would have its eastern terminus at or near the mutual borders of those three states. Davis gave command of its survey to Lieutenant Amiel Weeks Whipple.

The fourth and southernmost route, the one favored by Davis himself and many others from the Deep South, proceeded along roughly the 32nd parallel, near the border with Mexico. Davis sent two teams to explore it; one, under the command of Captain John B. Pope, working its way westward, the other, under Lieutenant John G. Parke, moving eastward.

The four Pacific Railroad Surveys were a superb achievement, in many ways the high point of army exploration of the West, and they served in some aspects as a prototype for the great surveys still to come. Their objective, as the historian Herman Viola has pointed out, was "not to map out the exact routes the railroads would follow, but rather to collect information about the climate, soil, rocks, minerals, and natural history of each route, as well as estimate engineering difficulties, economic potential, and the availability of such necessities for railroads of the time as water and timber." The army engineers were aided in their work by doctors, astronomers, meteorologists, geologists, botanists, naturalists, cartographers, and artists; "never before," according to the historian Henry Savage, "had any significant area of the country been so thoroughly and systematically subjected to the inspection of so many trained observers." The surveys' work was beautifully recorded in a series of 13 lavish volumes published between 1854 and 1859, which together constituted "an encyclopedia of western experience." Among the significant legacies of the Pacific Railroad Surveys was the creation by Lieutenant Gouverneur Kemble Warren of the

Lieutenant Gouverneur Kemble Warren's 1857 map of the West, which accompanied the Pacific Railroad Reports. *Warren's map drew on virtually all the exploratory work done to date in the West and was essentially the first scientifically based comprehensive map of the entire region.*

first scientifically accurate comprehensive map of the West—perhaps the most important cartographic representation of the West ever drawn.

As the determinant of the ultimate route of the transcontinental railroad, however, the surveys were a failure. The work of Lieutenant Edward Beckwith, who succeeded Gunnison as commander of the 38th parallel operation after he and several others were ambushed and killed by Paiute Indians along the Sevier River, actually anticipated the eventual path of the railroad, but all five survey commanders argued that their route was the most suitable.

MAP OF THE
TERRITORY OF THE UNITED STATES
FROM THE
MISSISSIPPI TO THE PACIFIC OCEAN

Davis, perhaps not surprisingly, tended to credit the arguments of Pope and Parke and concluded that "the route of the thirty-second parallel is, of those surveyed, 'the most practicable and economical route for a railroad from the Mississippi River to the Pacific Ocean.' " While conceding that the sectional interests of the South had been a factor in his decision, he denied that they had been paramount. "If the section of which I am a citizen has the best route, I ask who that looks to the interest of the country has a right to deny it the road," he explained to Congress in 1858.

But Davis's decision provoked dissension within the South, where a host of Mississippi River cities vied with one another to become the railway's eastern terminus, and the transcontinental railroad project proceeded no further for several years, until the South's secession from the Union in 1861 essentially removed sectional considerations from the question of western expansion. With the representatives of the southern states no longer present in Congress, western measures that just a short time earlier would have been the subject of endless debate were now easily passed.

Thus, on July 1, 1862, President Abraham Lincoln signed into law the Pacific Railway Act. This measure awarded the right to construct the transcontinental railroad to the Union Pacific Railroad, which was to build westward from Council Bluffs, Iowa, and to the Central Pacific Railroad, which was to build eastward from Sacramento, California. The railroad would follow one of the proposed northern routes, approximating roughly the 38th parallel route surveyed by Gunnison and Beckwith. From west to east, it would cross the Sierra Nevada through the Donner Pass, wend north of the Great Salt Lake, traverse the Wasatch range near the Weber River, proceed north of the Uinta Mountains, eventually cross the Rockies through the yet (as of 1862) to be discovered Evans (Lone Tree) Pass, and follow the South Platte and Platte rivers to the

Mississippi and its eastern terminus at Omaha, Nebraska, just across the river from Council Bluffs.

The transcontinental railroad would take seven years and the labor of thousands of men, many of them Civil War veterans or Chinese or Irish immigrants, to complete, and it would transform the West. Soon, Congress granted charters to three other corporations to construct transcontinental railways. With these charters were given huge land grants, which allowed the railways to sell cheap land and attract settlers along their routes. The coming of the railroads meant that crops and other goods could now be easily

transported to market; by the end of the Civil War, thousands of emigrants were flocking westward. Many were newly arrived immigrants from northern and western Europe; others were longer settled Americans fleeing the bloodshed and turmoil in the East or simply looking for new opportunities in the West.

Another 1862 act of Congress, the Homestead Act, which in earlier days most likely also would have fallen victim to southern opposition, also greatly stimulated western settlement. It granted 160 acres of western public lands to any homesteader who resided on it for 5 years; such

General John S. Casement stands guard over his supply train in Wyoming in 1868, at what was then the westernmost point of construction of the Union Pacific Railroad. In their haste to outdo the Central Pacific Railroad in the completion of the transcontinental railroad, workers on the Union Pacific were then laying track westward at the rate of eight miles per day.

land could also be purchased for $1.25 an acre after one had resided on it for 6 months. Its effect on western settlement was immediate. In 1864, the Reverend Jonathan Blanchard wrote of Council Bluffs, one of the most popular jumping-off points for western emigrants:

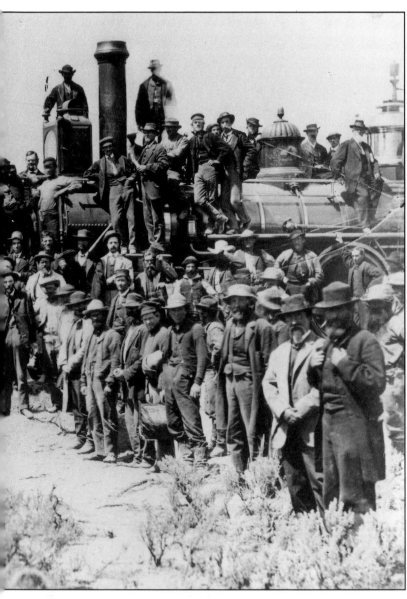

Chief engineer Samuel Montague (left) of the Central Pacific shakes hands with his counterpart, Grenville Dodge of the Union Pacific, as the rails are joined at Promontory, Utah, on May 10, 1869, marking the completion of the transcontinental railroad.

When you approach this town, the ravines and gorges are white with covered wagons at rest. Below the town, toward the river side, long wings of white canvas stretch away on either side, into the soft green willows; at the ferry from a quarter to a half mile of teams all the time await their turn

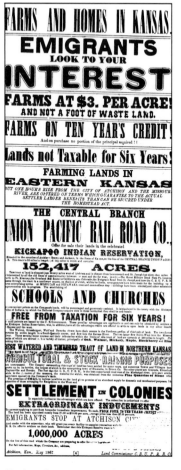

Railroad companies played an active role in encouraging settlement of the West, as this 1867 Union Pacific flyer illustrates. The Union Pacific is offering untaxed land at $3 an acre, no money down; the real estate, the "best watered and timbered tract of land in northern Kansas," lies in the "celebrated Kickapoo Indian reservation."

to cross. Myriads of horses and mules drag on the moving mass of humanity toward the setting sun; while the oxen and cows equal them in number.

And if one did not wish to till the soil, there were other reasons to go west. In 1849, the discovery of gold at Sutter's Mill, California, had triggered the first outbreak of what would be a recurring western contagion—gold fever. Thousands of "forty-niners," many by way of the lengthy sea journey around the southern tip of South America, flocked to California to dig and pan for the precious metal. Though few actually got rich, many stayed, settling down to farm in California's rich Central Valley or starting business enterprises. By 1852, the state's non-Indian population had increased thirteenfold, to more than 200,000; the influx formed the nucleus of a permanent population that would grow rapidly in the years to come.

This phenomenon would repeat itself several times in other regions of the West in succeeding years. In 1859, gold was discovered in the foothills of the Rockies near Pikes Peak in Colorado. Boomtowns such as Denver, Golden, Boulder, and Colorado City sprang up with amazing rapidity; Pikes Peak or Bust became the motto of countless pioneers. That same year silver was found on the eastern slopes of the Sierra Nevada, in what would become the state of Nevada; the next year gold was found in the easternmost portion of the Washington Territory, a region from which the territory and state of Idaho would soon be carved. In the 1870s, huge copper lodes were struck in Arizona. At each location, explosive population growth followed. Only a handful got rich, but the mere prospect of wealth enticed many west, and most of those stayed.

The speed with which the West was being settled at this time in many ways exceeded the overburdened federal government's capacity to deal with the situation, but with the Civil War over, sectional rivalries eliminated as a consideration in the settlement of the West, and Washington's primacy at the expense of the states and the territories

firmly established, new government attention was focused on the western lands. And there was much to be done if settlement was to proceed apace. Most of the region remained to be organized politically and brought to statehood. The general dimensions of the West were known and had been mapped, but the gold and silver strikes had indicated the importance of knowing not only the contours of the land but what lay beneath its surface. The Indians had to be pacified, driven off, or exterminated to make way for American settlement. New technologies, specifically in the agricultural sphere, had to be developed for use in the western environment, and questions concerning for what use the western lands were best suited remained to be answered. For all these reasons, a more comprehensive exploration of the West than any to date was a necessity; the region had been, in the words of the eminent

The Chrisman sisters pose outside their sod house on a homestead tract in Custer County, Nebraska. Those who took advantage of the Homestead Act to obtain 160-acre tracts on the Great Plains found that their land was seldom well watered or well timbered; in fact, wood suitable for use as building material was so rare on the prairies that houses made of sod were the norm.

historian Daniel Boorstin, "settled before it was explored."

With the war ended, the government had the wherewithal to pursue such a venture, and it was particularly blessed in terms of the human resources at its disposal. Between 1867 and 1879 it sponsored four comprehensive surveys of the American West, led by four remarkable men: Clarence King, a young, energetic, ambitious scientist whom his friend Henry Adams, the foremost 19th-century American historian, called the "best and brightest man of his generation"; George Montague Wheeler, a hard-driving army officer eager for the service to recover its leading role in the exploration of the West and anxious to gain the honor and glory that he had missed out on in the Civil War; Ferdinand Vandeveer Hayden, a self-made man, physician by training, scientist by inclination, a tireless promoter of himself and the West whom the Indians called Man-Who-Picks-Up-Stones-Running; and perhaps the greatest of them all, John Wesley Powell, who despite having lost his right arm at the Battle of Shiloh became the first white man to travel the length of the Colorado

River, running the rapids of the Grand Canyon in the process, and went on to propose a revolutionary new way of understanding the western lands. These four were aided in their work by a host of equally remarkable individuals, among them the photographers John H. Hillers, Timothy O'Sullivan, and William Henry Jackson; the artists Thomas Moran and William H. Holmes; and the scientists Clarence Dutton, James Terry Gardner, and Grove Karl Gilbert. Taken as a whole, the work of the four great surveys constituted the most complete and thoroughly documented examination of the West to date—its past, its present, and its future; its landscape, its climate, and its inhabitants. The surveys encompassed rollicking outdoor adventures and the soberest scientific analysis; grizzly bear attacks, freak thunderstorms, flash floods, forest fires, Indian fights, and political infighting and backstabbing in the corridors of Washington; a jewel hoax, a score of new discoveries, and some of the most stunning artistic visions of the West ever recorded. Most significantly, they would forever change the way Americans understand the West.

John Hillers, who did his most important work with John Wesley Powell's U.S. Geological and Geographical Survey of the Rocky Mountains, took this photograph of the beehive geysers on the Firehole River in what is today Yellowstone National Park. The four great government-sponsored surveys of the American West that took to the field in the years following the Civil War did more than any previous exploratory expeditions to document the western lands.

The Best
and Brightest

He was only 25 years old when he was given command of the U.S. Geological Exploration of the Fortieth Parallel in 1867, and his appointment anointed him as the golden boy of American science. "Now, Mr. King," Secretary of War Edwin Stanton said as he handed him his commission as geologist in charge of the survey, "the sooner you get out of Washington, the better—you are too young a man to be seen about town with this appointment in your pocket—there are four major-generals who want your place." He enjoyed the friendship and support of the titans of the American scientific community—Louis Agassiz, the Swiss-born Harvard professor who had recently completed the fourth volume of *Contributions to the Natural History of the United States* and was perhaps America's greatest naturalist; James Dwight Dana, the nation's foremost geologist, who as a much younger man had made his mark as one of the "scientifics" with Charles Wilkes's South Seas Exploring Expedition; Josiah Dwight Whitney, the head of the great mineralogical survey of California that served as the model for King's project and had given him his first taste of scientific work; William H. Brewer, Whitney's most trusted and talented colleague, who had overseen most of the fieldwork of the California Survey; Spencer Fullerton Baird, zoologist and secretary of the United States's national museum, the Smithsonian Institution, who was attempting to complete a comprehensive catalog of all the wildlife of the West.

The great photographer of the West, William Henry Jackson, composes his shot of California's breathtaking Yosemite Valley from atop Glacier Point. Jackson, who clambered to many such a precarious perch as photographer with the Hayden survey, said that a successful picture requires "labor, patience, and moral stamina." He could have said the same about the qualities required of a survey leader.

To Henry Adams, his great friend's appointment, despite the plethora of personal characteristics and qualifications that recommended him for the job, always remained something of a mystery and was one more indication that King had been specially favored by fortune. "It is not necessary," Adams wrote in 1871, as the Fortieth Parallel Survey was in the midst of its work, "to investigate by what 'happy accident' it was brought about that a work of such importance should be inaugurated, or how it came to be placed in charge of a competent person, and carried on uninterruptedly until important results had been obtained." For Adams, who often despaired at the prevalence of corruption and graft in postwar Washington, such happy accidents as the one that matched King's abilities with the tasks to be carried out by the Fortieth Parallel Survey occurred all too seldom. The West, for Adams, as he recorded in his famous autobiography, *The Education of Henry Adams*, was the "land of the future"; the men of the survey "held under their hammers a thousand miles of mineral country with all its riddles to solve, and its stores of possible wealth to mark. They felt the future in their hands." The congressional act enabling the survey to begin its work, with King at its head, therefore represented for Adams the "first modern act of legislation."

Adams was the quintessential Washington insider, the scion of one of America's first families, the son of a diplomat, the great-grandson of the nation's second president, the grandson of its sixth, friend to congressmen and confidant of cabinet secretaries, but his proximity to power made him also privy to the compromises and corrupt bargains that lubricated the wheels of state: the horse trading of votes in exchange for favors and influence, the bribery and graft endemic to Washington, the ways in which questions of national importance were made beholden to narrow regional, corporate, and even personal interests. The result was a profound ambivalence on Adams's part toward the American experiment with democracy as it was enacted

in Washington, an alternating (and sometimes simulta-
neous) fascination with and distaste for the way the system
operated.

But to Adams, King seemed untainted, as fresh as the
clear mountain air of the Colorado Rockies that Adams
breathed in 1871 on his first trip West. Although an easterner by birth and just four years younger than Adams,
King seemed of a different, newer generation, untouched
by the partisanship that Adams disdained, his destiny
linked with the wide open spaces across the Mississippi,
possessed of what his friend called "Californian instincts."
Most important of all, King was a man of science through
and through. "The lines of their lives converged," Adams
wrote, "but King had moulded and directed his life logi-
cally, scientifically, as Adams thought American life
should be directed." Surely science, with its emphasis on
impartiality and rationality, once brought to bear on the

*Ever the dandy, Clarence King
(in derby hat, seated at left)
often dressed for dinner even
while in camp with his survey.
The collapse of King's fortunes in
later life would lead some to
criticize him as a man too fond
of money and pleasure, but to
Americans such as the historian
Henry Adams, King's youthful
character seemed the perfect blend
of elegance and toughness, dash
and sobriety, literary intuition
and scientific rationality.*

organization of the western lands, with all their resources, richness, and promise, would offer American society as a whole some direction for its future course, believed Adams and like-minded individuals. And according to Adams, there could hardly be anyone more well suited for any challenge than King, whose virtues were those of his nation:

> His wit and humor; his bubbling energy which swept every one into the current of his interest; his personal charm of youth and manners; his faculty of giving and taking, profusely, lavishly, whether in thought or in money as though he was Nature herself, marked him almost alone among Americans. . . . No other American approached him for the combination of chances—physical energy, social standing, mental scope and training, wit, geniality, and science, that seemed superlatively American and irresistibly strong.

Clarence Rivers King had seemed destined for great things since his youth. He was born in Newport, Rhode Island, on January 6, 1842. Although in later life he would frequently express an elitist view of society—"I wish it could be intimated in my life and engraved on my tombstone that I am to the last fibre aristocratic in belief, that I think the only fine thing to do with the masses is to govern and educate them into some fine semblance of their social superiors," he wrote a friend—his own ancestry was not exceptionally distinguished. His most notable relative was a great-grandfather who was reputed to have been a friend of Benjamin Franklin's and a minor inventor in his own right. King's father, a trader in silks and tea for the East Indian mercantile firm of Talbot, Oliphant and Company, died in the Chinese port city of Amoy when his only child was just six years old. As a boy, King's closest friend and most frequent companion was his mother, who encouraged his interest in the natural world and in collecting stones and fossils. In a very short time, he turned the small apartment he and his mother occupied into a "veritable museum," according to his future colleague and biographer Samuel Franklin Emmons.

Despite the financial difficulty that followed the death of King's father and the 1857 bankruptcy of his trading firm, in which virtually all of the family's money was invested, Florence King saw to it that her son received a first-rate education. He attended preparatory school in Hartford, Connecticut, before enrolling in the Sheffield Scientific School of Yale University. Sheffield was the province of only the most advanced students; in the words of William H. Goetzmann, it "served the function of a graduate school and a place for special advanced work with the great men of the day."

It was at Yale that King's light first began to blaze. Many of the nation's most prominent scientists served on the Sheffield School's faculty, and King quickly became a favorite student, equally at home in the field or classroom, a writer of "delicate literary judgment and skill" according to a classmate. A fellow student remembered later that King was at that time "alert, independent, quick to receive impressions, ready to act on his own impulses, fond of literature and science, with that token of genius which is said to be 'the art of lighting one's own fires.'" He excelled at nonacademic pursuits as well; although somewhat on the short side, he possessed a robust physique and boundless energy and was a herculean rower. He had already begun to demonstrate those multiple traits of character that drew people to him and that are often collectively and loosely defined as charisma. Henry Adams would characterize the feeling that King's friends felt for him as "worship" for the "ideal American that they all wanted to be" but wrote that the scientist was "so little egoistic . . . that none of his friends felt envy of his extraordinary superiority." King was himself becoming modestly aware of the force of his personality. "Don't think that I never lead men, for in my own humble way I do," he wrote his great friend and schoolmate James Terry Gardner in March

Henry Adams, the descendant of some of America's Founding Fathers, believed King to be the embodiment of a new type of ideal American, supremely equipped to lead his nation into a new era. He remained loyal to King throughout the troubles that marred his last years. Although others found King's fall symbolic of a grasping and corrupt age too devoted to the superficial pursuit of wealth, Adams believed it to be the tragedy of a man endowed with insufficient material means to fulfill his ambitious vision.

1862, near the end of his stay at the Sheffield School. "I can see my influence in college plainly enough. I am happy here. I am loved by some people, and that is happiness."

If to Adams, King seemed the ideal of a new American, it was perhaps due in part to his seeming untouched by that most critical and corrosive event of 19th-century American history, the Civil War. In the summer of 1862, King was a member of the first class to be awarded bachelor of science degrees from the Sheffield School. But while young men were fighting and the guns were blazing on the Chickahominy River, at Manassas, at Antietam, at Vicksburg, and at Fredericksburg, King, with three friends, including Gardner, was rowing Lake Champlain, on the border of New York and Vermont, and the St. Lawrence River all the way to Quebec city. That next winter he spent in further scientific study and dabbling in painting. Then he decided to make his way overland to California with Gardner, ostensibly in the hope that the warm weather and sunshine there would help restore his friend's failing health, although a cross-country journey, which was at the time still a rather rugged undertaking, was hardly the prescribed tonic for an overtaxed constitution.

The trip, which took up most of the summer of 1863, was every bit the adventure that the two young easterners had hoped for. At St. Joseph, Missouri, they bought horses and gear and hooked up with a wagon train headed for California. Thirteen miles west, at the frontier settlement of Troy, Kansas, they were reminded that even in the West it was impossible to escape the nation's problems when a party of rugged Kansans accused the greenhorns of kidnapping blacks and running them to Missouri to be sold into slavery. Fortunately, the wagon train's leader, a veteran of the trail named Speers, intervened on their behalf, and the party continued westward, following the Platte River for much of its journey. After a layover at Fort Laramie, the party proceeded up the Sweetwater River, where King was impressed by the massive herds of buffalo it encountered. Impulsively, he traded his horse for a buffalo pony and rode it into the thundering herd's midst, but his first shot at a huge bull only wounded the shaggy beast, which then charged its assailant. A butt from its massive horned head crushed the rib cage of King's mount, which toppled over in pain, pinning its rider beneath it. More experienced hands quickly rode to the easterner's rescue, saving him more serious injury. As it was, King limped for a while and had to remain behind for a day or two before catching up with the wagon train via stagecoach. His horse was less fortunate; it had to be destroyed.

The emigrants and their scientific companions crossed the Rockies at South Pass, the famous mountain crossing "discovered" by the mountain men in the early 19th century. On the far side of the great range, King had his first glimpse of the region that would command most of his attention in the West—the Great Basin, as the desert land, punctuated by mountains, between California's Sierra Nevada and the Wasatch Mountains is known. At the Humboldt River, King and Gardner bid farewell to the wagon train; after a short stay in Virginia City, a quintessential freewheeling mining boom town, they hiked on foot over the rugged Sierra Nevada into California and on to Sacramento and a river voyage to San Francisco.

While aboard their river steamer, King and Gardner had a fortunate encounter. Gardner was studying his fellow passengers, most of whom were miners, rough-hewn types for the most part, clad in jeans, flannel, and boots, long-barreled revolvers holstered at their hips. One of these gentlemen in particular caught his eye. He looked much like the others, with his "old felt hat, a quick eye, a sunburned face . . . a long weatherbeaten neck protruding from a coarse gray flannel shirt and a rough coat, a heavy revolver belt and long legs," yet Gardner was convinced that "this man was different," that he was an "intellectual man." Upon striking up a conversation with the stranger, Gardner learned that his supposition had been accurate; his conversational partner was none other than William H. Brewer, once of the Sheffield School and now Josiah Dwight Whitney's top assistant on the California Geological Survey. In just a short time, Brewer had offered King a position with the survey. (Gardner took a job in San Francisco with the army topographic corps, but he soon tired of it and also hired on with the survey.)

King would spend the next 4 years with Whitney's survey, which in its 10 years of existence (1860–70) would accomplish prodigies of scientific exploration. Whitney's team succeeded in mapping the entire state in meticulous detail, examining much of its known mineral deposits, uncovering its geological past, and making recommendations for its agricultural development. The survey would serve in many ways as the prototype for even more extensive scientific examinations of the West, and for King, who worked for Whitney as a geologist and topographer, it would serve as a training ground on which to prepare himself for the ambitious project he was already planning—a scientific survey of the Great Basin, the "vast loneliness" of which, according to Gardner, had fascinated the two Yale men on their way west. Perhaps the most lasting legacy of the California Survey resulted from Whitney's proposal to President Lincoln that he grant the breathtaking Yosemite Valley to the state of California as a public park. This idea, with which Lincoln concurred, foreshadowed the creation of a national park system—the setting aside by the federal government of the nation's most spectacular wilderness areas for the perpetual enjoyment of the American public.

For King, the California Geological Survey seems also to have been a great adventure and tremendous fun. He spent most of his time scaling mountain peaks at the "top of California," in the Sierra Nevada, "a long and massive uplift lying between the arid deserts of the Great Basin and the Californian exuberance of grain-field and orchard; its eastern slope, a defiant wall of rock plunging abruptly down to the plain; the western, a long, grand sweep, well watered and overgrown with cool stately forests; its crest a line of sharp, snowy peaks springing into the sky and catching the alpenglow long after the sun has set for the rest of America." (The quoted material is from King's *Mountaineering in the Sierra Nevada,* as his collection of accounts of these years was called when it was published in book

form in 1872. A brilliant achievement, the book is a narrative, sometimes fictionalized treatment of his California
escapades rather than a scientific treatise and reveals yet
another aspect of King's multifaceted genius.)

As a scientist, King had a little bit of Indiana Jones in
him. His published scholarly work was exceptional and
groundbreaking in its day, but he seems to have been most
himself when prowling the wild. A sophisticate and a bon
vivant; a witty, scintillating conversationalist; a connois-
seur of art and literature; the confidant of Adams and, in
later years, of the great American novelist Henry James,
with whom he visited several of Europe's most dazzling
capital cities, King could sometimes be found relaxing at
the end of the day in a camp chair at some dusty frontier
outpost dressed to the nines in derby hat, cravat, waistcoat,
dinner jacket, and tailored trousers with piping along the
sides, but a more characteristic pose was the one captured
by Timothy O'Sullivan in his well-known 1867 photograph: King wedged in a crevice on some precipitous slope,
his hold secured by a rope snaking down from above and
out of the frame. The mountaineer looks jaunty and confident, rather pleased with himself. "King is enthusiastic,
is wonderfully tough, has the greatest endurance I've ever
seen, and is withal very muscular. He is a most perfect
specimen of health," wrote Brewer in 1864.

Such a dynamo could not work for someone else for
long, and King began dreaming of heading his own survey
soon after joining Whitney's team. He and Gardner often
discussed such plans, and both of them became convinced
that one could understand the geology of the West only
through careful study of the "structure, topographical and
geographical, of the whole mountain system of western
America from the Plains to the Pacific." On a summer
day in 1866, while the two friends were gazing east across
the Great Basin from the peak of Mount Conners in the
Sierra Nevada, the structure for his survey took shape in
King's mind. In a matter of months, armed with letters of

recommendation from some of the most eminent American men of science, he was in Washington, D.C., calling on patrons and potential backers and surprising everyone by securing from the War Department the much-coveted appointment to head the Fortieth Parallel Survey.

Brigadier General Andrew A. Humphreys, a veteran of the Army Corps of Topographical Engineers and the army officer assigned the responsibility of overseeing the survey,

Clarence King in his beloved Sierra Nevada, as captured by survey photographer Timothy O'Sullivan. "Nature in her present aspects, as well as in the records of her past, here constantly offers the most vivid and terrible contrasts. Can anything be more wonderfully opposite than that period of leaden sky, gray granite, and desolate stretches of white?" wrote King in Mountaineering in the Sierra Nevada.

allowed King to write his own orders over Humphreys's signature. They remain the clearest statement of the expedition's ambitious scope:

> The object of the exploration is to examine and describe the geological structure, geographical condition and natural resources of a belt of country extending from the 120th meridian to the 105th meridian, along the 40th parallel of latitude with sufficient expansion north and south to include the line of the "Central" and "Union Pacific" railroads. . . . The exploration will be commenced at the 120th meridian where it will connect with the geological survey of California. . . . It should examine all rock formations, mountain ranges, detrital plains, coal deposits, soils, minerals, ores, saline and alkaline deposits . . . collect . . . material for a topographical map of the regions traversed . . . conduct . . . barometric and thermometric observations [and] make collections in botany and zoology with a view to a memoir on these subjects.

In short, King proposed to explore and map, using newly developed and more accurate techniques, a 100-mile swath (north to south) along the route of the transcontinental railroad from the Sierra Nevada to the Rocky Mountains. The mapping work was important, but it was a secondary priority to King's geological excavations.

To the layman, geology—the science of the earth's history, composition, and structure—can often seem the most baffling and arcane of intellectual pursuits, but in the post–Civil War United States it was often viewed as being at the cutting edge of scientific investigation, for both theoretical and practical reasons. With its promise of revealing the secrets of the earth's creation, geology seemed to offer as well insight into the very nature of existence, much as theoretical physics has been viewed as doing in our century. In the same way that in the late 19th century proponents of so-called Social Darwinism used their interpretation of Charles Darwin's controversial theory of evolution to explain societal relationships—it was argued, for example, that certain individuals accumulated wealth and power because they were the "fittest" of their species— fundamental geological tenets were seen as having profound implications for the understanding of society and history.

The most elemental and heated geological debate concerned the opposing theories of uniformitarianism and catastrophism. Adherents of the former believed that the earth developed through uniform, cyclical progressions; adherents of the latter held that catastrophes—earthquakes, volcanic eruptions, floods—were the most crucial shapers of the earth. In looking at human affairs, a uniformitarian might be inclined to view a cataclysm such as the Civil War, for example, as a ghastly aberration in the course of human development, the likes of which should be at all cost avoided in the future; a catastrophist might view it as an inevitable, necessary upheaval, no matter how costly, that made future progress possible.

But it was geology's more practical applications that excited most of those concerned with western settlement, for among the rocks, minerals, and liquefied elements a geologist might uncover in the course of his survey were gold, silver, copper, coal, iron, and oil—building materials and fuels for a rapidly industrializing nation and individual financial empires. Although always a man of science, King did not repeat the mistake made by his mentor Whitney, who scorned the requests of California's legislators and business titans that he pay particular attention to mineral deposits because to do so would turn his survey into a "mere prospecting expedition." Consequently, in the later years of his survey Whitney faced a constant struggle for funds, as politicians and captains of industry wondered why his men could succeed in uncovering countless fossil remains of prehistoric creatures but manage to overlook the rich oil fields near Santa Barbara. King never lost sight of who controlled his purse strings, and

he was always adept at cultivating and stroking the congressmen and lobbyists who could make the difference
regarding appropriations.

King was also sensitive to strategic considerations. It was
no coincidence that he proposed that his survey follow the
course of the transcontinental railroad, for he recognized
that the railroad would stimulate settlement and economic

development; without the railroad, it was doubtful that anyone in Washington would have been overly interested in a geological survey of the Great Basin, for it was simply too remote and forbidding a region. The railroad was also critical to the army's plans for pacifying the Indian population of the West—the military regarded the railroad and the settlement that would accompany it as the wedge

A Union Pacific locomotive crosses a temporary trestle near Citadel Rock at Green River, Wyoming, in late 1868. King shrewdly proposed that his survey of the Great Basin follow roughly the path of the transcontinental railroad, recognizing that the government and business interests would be most immediately concerned with the western lands traversed by the railroad.

that would finally force the Indians from their lands—and the Fortieth Parallel Survey was under the military's auspices.

In July 1867, King established his first base camp in the field near the Truckee River and the settlement of Glendale, not far from the present-day city of Reno, Nevada. With him there on the edge of the vast alkali flats of the Nevada desert were most of the key members of his scientific team, many of whom were, like King, young easterners—Gardner, who served as topographer and field leader when King was absent, was King's age; the brothers James Duncan Hague and Arnold Hague, geologists, were 31 and 26; the geologist Samuel Franklin Emmons was 26; and the botanist William Whitman Bailey was just 24. Other important members of the party were the ornithologist Robert Ridgway; the botanist Sereno Watson, a 42-year-old failure at 6 different professions who wandered into camp one day and asked for a job; and the topographer Henry Custer. All were civilians; given the chance to pick his own staff, King had included no one from the Army Corps of Engineers (the successor to the topographic corps). The only real military aspect of the survey was the escort of cavalry troopers that guarded the scientists' safety. A shifting number of paid civilian assistants—mule skinners, packers, cooks, and hunters—also accompanied the survey, which all in all usually numbered between 40 and 50 people.

One of the survey members destined to be longest remembered was the photographer Timothy O'Sullivan. During the Civil War, the pictures taken by the great Mathew Brady and his team of able assistants proved incontrovertibly photography's documentary value, and in the decades following the war, photography, still a relatively new technique in the United States, would enjoy enormous popularity. Painters and artists were regularly employed by exploratory expeditions to make a visual record of their discoveries, but King and the leaders of the

three other great surveys were among the first explorers to make use of the camera eye. The photographs of the great surveys proved invaluable not only as scientific documentation and artistic statement—and they are some of the greatest photographs of the West ever taken—but also as publicity for the surveys. The public flocked to exhibits where they were shown (often alongside paintings of the same vistas, for the surveys also employed artists; King's party, for example, was joined by the landscape painter Gilbert Munger in 1869), and no gift was more likely, as King and his counterparts soon learned, to flatter a congressman and win his support for additional appropriations as a set of the most recent photographic plates from the western surveys. O'Sullivan had himself worked for Brady, and although his never-ending stream of war stories sometimes exasperated his camp mates—"One would think he

Timothy O'Sullivan's mule-drawn darkroom, a former Civil War ambulance, crosses the lonely dunes southwest of Carson Sink, Nevada, in the Great Basin. O'Sullivan's greatest western photographs were usually pure landscapes; in this case the footprints leading away from the comparatively small wagon and frail-looking mules emphasize the barren grandeur and power of the land in the face of man's intrusion.

had slept with Grant and Meade [the hero of the Union victory at the Battle of Gettysburg] and was the direct confidant of Stanton," Bailey wrote—he was a popular member of the survey.

Initially, the survey's progress was slow, in part because it took time for the scientists—tenderfeet, many of them— to acclimate themselves to the practical aspects of western campaigning. Among the most problematic of these was the singular temperament of the survey's mules, which were used as mounts and beasts of burden as well as to pull supply wagons. Although much better suited than horses for the work load, climate, and rugged terrain, the beasts were ornery and stubborn and seemed to take a mulish delight in bedeviling their handlers by refusing to hold still to be loaded in the morning or finding some ingenious way to rid themselves of all or part of their burden of supplies, such as intentionally brushing against a tree trunk or the outcroppings of some narrow mountain pass. Nor were they particularly comfortable mounts. "I take a little ride every day on mule back," Bailey complained in correspondence to his brother from the first base camp, "and am at present afflicted with a most grievous tail. . . . King says for my comfort there is no bum on earth but will get hardened to it." (The members of each of the four surveys had similar complaints about their mules, although all concerned nevertheless recognized the animals as being indispensable.)

The scientists had to learn in a hurry, for the region they were to survey was an extremely challenging environment, according to King "in every way the most difficult and dangerous country to campaign in . . . on the continent." Most of the Great Basin along or near the 40th parallel is exceedingly desolate. It receives very little rainfall, and summertime temperatures can be tremendously high, but it is not the flat desert of common misconception. Between the Sierra Nevada and the Wasatch Mountains, which roughly mark its western and eastern extent, rise, in Sereno Watson's words, "numerous short and somewhat isolated minor ranges." These mountains generally run north to south and are divided by broad valleys. Most of the land is parched and alkaline; wildlife is relatively scarce, and in King's time, as today, human inhabitants were few and far between. The most frequently encountered denizens were jackrabbits, coyotes, snakes, tarantulas, scorpions, and vultures; wagon wheels, the bleached bones of oxen, discarded furniture, and the lonesome, crudely marked graves of departed pioneers testified that the Great Basin had been a boulevard of broken dreams for more than one emigrant family on its way west.

In mid-July 1867 the Fortieth Parallel Survey set out into this desolate wasteland. Typically, King, who had devoted much time and thought to, in his words, "initiating a good system of fieldwork and planning work for the parties," selected the site for a base camp, where tents were raised, either in parallel rows or in a square. An American flag was usually raised overhead along with the official flag of the survey. These camps served as a sort of central headquarters for anywhere from a couple of weeks to several months; from them, on King's instructions, various field parties fanned out into the surrounding countryside. Bailey, Watson, and Ridgway, the botanists and the ornithologist, usually stayed closest to home in their forays for flora and fauna specimens, while the topographers and geologists ranged farther afield. Most parties consisted of two or three scientists, a cook, and a packer, who aided in the loading and unloading of the always recalcitrant mules. Often a party would be accompanied by a cavalry detachment for protection from the Indians, although many of the scientists regarded the soldiers as more hindrance than help.

In this way, a relatively small number of men were able to complete a large number of scientific tasks. In the survey's first season alone—the last field party came into winter headquarters at Virginia City, Nevada, on December

Clarence King's West, as captured by Timothy O'Sullivan: Salt Lake City and the Wasatch Mountains of Utah.

24—it covered a huge chunk of territory between 41 and 39 degrees north latitude, reaching from the California-Nevada border as far east as the second Humboldt mountain range. Using what became known as the American system of surveying, which involved the use of readings taken from mountain peaks and complicated mathematical calculations verified by astronomical measurements, King and his surveyors made the beginnings of the first comprehensive geodetic survey of the Great Basin. (Geodesy is a branch of applied mathematics concerned with fixing the exact location of various points on the earth's surface. The purpose of the type of surveying that King and his men were carrying out was to enable the subsequent creation of extremely precise and detailed maps on which the

location of relatively small geographic landmarks and features—a specific mountain or stream—were precisely indicated.) In the process, such significant geographic
features as the Truckee Mountains, Pyramid Lake, and
the Humboldt River were explored in great detail.

Scientific surveying is extremely painstaking work,
much more easily summarized than accomplished. In the
summer of 1867, temperatures in the Great Basin often
exceeded 100°F, and an unusually wet winter and spring
had turned the Humboldt Sink and Carson Sink areas—
a sink is a depression in a land surface, often in the area
of a lake—into pestilential swamps. The hardy few inhabitants of the Humboldt Sink area, where the survey
spent much of its time that year, characterized it as the
"worst place between Missouri and hell." A demented
wandering hermit echoed such sentiment, to the unease
of the intrepid surveyors: "Desolation, thy name is Humboldt," he solemnly intoned over and over. This godfor-
saken area bred illness, and by early September virtually
every member of the party, which including cavalry escort
then numbered about 50, had been stricken by malaria,
known locally as the "mountain ail." King later wrote
Humphreys that at one point only three men, including
himself, remained well enough to continue working.

Determined to persevere, King personally carried on the
survey of the Stillwater Range, just east of the Carson Sink,
in central Nevada. While sighting through his theodolite
(a standard surveying tool) aboard a peak in that range,
King was struck by lightning. "I was staggered and my
brain nerves severely shocked," he reported to Humphreys;
the bolt left the right side of his body a charred brown for
several weeks. Illness and lightning were but two mani-
festations of the hardship that the scientists had to over-
come daily; others included heat so searing that the
scientists in desperation sought shelter in the slim shadow
thrown by a telegraph pole or by their mule and nightly
insect infestations during which the swarms were so thick

as to snuff out candles and lanterns and the exhausted, sweating men sometimes breathed in winged creatures with their air.

But even in winter quarters in Virginia City and Carson City, the survey continued its work. Near Virginia City, King, Emmons, and the Hagues investigated the Com-

A slope on Lone Peak Summit in the Wasatch Mountains, at the eastern end of the Great Basin. Photograph by O'Sullivan.

stock Lode, the richest vein of silver ever discovered on the continent. They were joined by O'Sullivan, whose photographs of the lode were the first such taken underground in the United States. Meanwhile, the other members of the scientific team collated their specimen collections and the topographers began working on their

maps, which were drawn initially at a scale of two miles to the inch.

In similar fashion, over the course of the next five years, the survey continued, overcoming countless daily obstacles and ultimately traversing the Rocky Mountains and reaching as far east as north-central Colorado. King had envisioned that the survey would remain in the field for only three years, but his "intense yearning" to complete his "analytical study of Nature and drink in the sympathetic side" fell victim to the survey's scientific, political, and popular success, as General Humphreys repeatedly ordered him and his men to extend their work.

King's investigation of the Comstock Lode paid the most immediate dividends. "I can unhesitatingly say that we have the most thorough account of any great silver mining district in the world," he wrote Humphreys in July 1868. In that same letter, he went on to predict that even greater silver reserves would be found at the untapped lower depths of the lode. This ran contrary to prevailing opinion, which was pessimistic regarding further exploitation of the mine, but King was proved right in 1874 when the richest vein of any in the Comstock Lode was struck. By that time, the survey's first publication, *The Mining Industry*, had appeared. Authored by King and James Duncan Hague, with contributions from Emmons, it was quickly recognized as the definitive work on the subject, and its immediate practical applications won King strong support in Congress. (By contrast, Whitney had never recovered from the political damage done him by his decision to make a volume on paleontology the first publication of his California survey; the work was handsome and useful but scorned by legislators as being of no practical value.) Of even greater interest was the discovery by Emmons and the Hagues of a new process by which to smelt the ore that contained silver. King's geologists estimated that the old process had wasted $40 million worth of silver from the Comstock Lode over the preceding 8 years, and they

A *miner seeks silver in the Comstock Lode. The candle in the foreground provided the only light at the end of this shaft; its guttering would also inform the miner that his oxygen level had grown perilously low. This photograph was one of a series taken by O'Sullivan in the Comstock Lode using a magnesium flare.*

hoped to raise the yield by 30 percent. King's team further endeared itself to those interested in mining by the discovery, in the summer of 1869, of huge coal fields in the Green River country west of the Wasatch Mountains.

During these years, King was as energetic and ebullient as ever, racing from field site to field site; riding the newly completed transcontinental railroad to winter in San Francisco, where he renewed his friendship with Bret Harte, the well-known writer of colorful tales of western life; making quick jaunts to Washington to lobby politicians and to New Haven to oversee the survey's publications. He remained a fascinating combination of the outdoorsman, the intellectual, and the dandy, a man who could outwit

A *member of the King survey, perhaps King himself, peers over the edge of a glacier in the Sierra Nevada. King would come to embrace catastrophe as the primary shaper of the earth and the environment. "Moments of great catastrophe, thus translated into the language of life, become moments of creation, when out of plastic organisms something new and nobler is called into being," King argued in 1877, but he would be unable to recover from the catastrophic ruin of his personal fortunes.*

Mexican bandits while whistling an aria from *La Traviata* to calm his spooked horse; who would chase a deserter from his cavalry escort 100 miles over baked Nevada desert and mountain before heading him off at a pass and pistol-whipping him into submission; who would crawl into a dark, musty cave, armed with only a single-shot rifle, after a wounded grizzly bear; who, impeccably attired in swallowtail coat and gloves, would in the most elegant parlors and dining rooms of the nation's capital impress fellow guests with his scintillating conversation, impeccable manners, and boundless charm. (Mrs. Henry Adams was just one of the distinguished women said to be in love with him.) In 1872, his literary promise, which Adams and others had commented on, was fulfilled by the publication of *Mountaineering in the Sierra Nevada*; although the

book may be marred, for the modern reader, by King's condescension toward those he deemed his social and racial inferiors, it remains a singular and skilled evocation of one of the West's natural wonders, impassioned, learned, and timeless. A year earlier, while climbing in the Sierra Nevada, King discovered the first active glacier in the United States. His find represented the quintessential King blend of the physical and the intellectual; an admirable mountaineering feat in itself, it enabled him to refute the claims of the most prominent geologists of the day, who believed there were no active glaciers within the continental United States, and to crystallize his understanding of the geological history of the West, which he attempted to reconstruct in his monumental *Systematic Geology*. King even helped preserve the confidence of the American investor through his role in exposing the Great Diamond Hoax, a scheme designed by two confidence men to convince America's leading financiers that a huge field of diamonds and emeralds had been discovered at an undisclosed location in the West.

With their encyclopedic knowledge of the West's geology, King and his men immediately recognized the unlikelihood of such a claim, and their unmatched familiarity with the West's topography enabled them to deduce that the so-called diamond field must be located near Brown's Hole, not far from the Green River near the conjunction of Colorado, Utah, and Wyoming. Their subsequent investigation of the area indeed yielded diamonds, but the field, as King was able to prove, had quite obviously been seeded by the charlatans in an attempt to fool investors. His exposure of the hoax, which had duped a syndicate of Western bankers and industrialists, made King a hero and won his survey even greater praise. "We have escaped, thanks to God and Clarence King, a great financial calamity," opined an editorial writer in the San Francisco *Chronicle*. The San Francisco *Bulletin* praised him as a "cool-headed man of scientific education . . .

[who] has done the public a memorable service, the mere statement of which carries with it all the praise a man like him can desire, as it is the only reward he will receive."

Such endeavors were enough to tax even the most heroic energies, and by the conclusion of the summer of 1873, when the survey at last finished its fieldwork, King was weary and ill. He quickly regrouped, however, for ahead of him still loomed the survey's most important work—the organization of the mountain of information it had gathered into the publications that would constitute its

ultimate scientific legacy. As always, King's ambition was grand: "The day has passed in geological science when it is either decent or tolerable to rush into print with undigested field operations ignoring the methods and appliances in use among advanced investigators," he wrote Humphreys in February 1874. "It is my intention to give to this work a finish which will place it on an equal footing with the best European publications, and those few which have redeemed the wavering reputation of our American investigators."

The Shoshone Falls from the south bank of the Snake River in southern Idaho. O'Sullivan regarded this photograph as one of his best; he called it "one of the most sublime of the Rocky Mountain scenes."

A New System of Examination

King's success was the military's dilemma. The army was justifiably proud of the achievements of its engineering corps in mapping and surveying the West, and it wished to regain its preeminence in terms of western exploration. King's survey was technically under the army's auspices and supervision, but it was for all intents and purposes a civilian affair, run by a civilian, manned by civilian scientists, devoted—as many officers saw it—to civilian aims. There were in addition two other surveys in the field at the same time as King's. Headed by John Wesley Powell and Ferdinand Hayden, these were clearly civilian affairs, run by the Department of the Interior. Western exploration had been one of the army's traditional peacetime projects, an activity useful in winning congressional appropriations and support. With its influence waning after the Civil War—the number of regular troops fell from 1 million to 25,000 between 1865 and 1867—the army desperately needed to regain its prestige. To that end, General Humphreys, although always supportive of King and his work, began searching for a talented officer who could lead the Army Corps of Engineers' own survey.

He found his man in 1869 in the person of First Lieutenant George Montague Wheeler, a 27-year-old native of Hopkinton, Massachusetts. Wheeler was one of the saddest of late-19th-century types, a career officer enamored of the army and desperate for glory who had been born just a little too late to take part in the Civil War. By

One of O'Sullivan's photographs of the ruined cliff dwellings of the Anasazi in Canyon de Chelly, in northeastern Arizona, which the U.S. Geological Surveys West of the One Hundredth Meridian, commanded by Lieutenant George Montague Wheeler, visited in 1875. The Anasazi culture, which produced the most elaborate native architecture in North America, vanished abruptly in the 13th century.

the time he received his commission from West Point in the spring of 1866—graduating sixth overall in his class but first in engineering—the guns had been silent for more than a year. Of course, one could always make one's reputation fighting Indians, but in the intense jockeying for desirable postings that accompanied the shrinking of the postwar army, the best positions seemed always to be reserved for Civil War veterans.

Still, Wheeler was not totally without prospects. His marriage to the daughter of Francis Preston Blair, Jr., former congressman, general of the Union under William Tecumseh Sherman, and vice-presidential candidate in the 1868 election, assured him of some pull, and he was promoted to first lieutenant and posted to the army's Department of California, where he was trained as a military topographer by Colonel R. S. Williamson, an Army Corps of Engineers veteran who had served on the railroad surveys and other exploratory forays. In 1868 and 1869, Wheeler explored some 82,000 square miles of the forbidding desert regions of southern Nevada and Utah, south of those surveyed by King and his colleagues. The primary purpose of this work was to find a practicable overland route for the transfer of troops southward from Idaho, Washington, Oregon, and northern Utah to Arizona and New Mexico. Previously, the army had marched such troops to Pacific ports in the Northwest, carried them south by ship to southern California, and then marched them overland again. It was during this time that Wheeler credited himself—a claim that has been disputed—with naming the great plateau region at the conjunction of Utah, Colorado, Arizona, and New Mexico the Colorado Plateau.

But as an explorer, as a soldier, Wheeler was too late. Even as he was taking the field and making tentative plans for a related investigation of the Colorado River, a region that he correctly claimed was yet to be "instrumentally explored," John Wesley Powell and eight companions were descending that spectacular watercourse in four

(continued on page 73)

Yosemite and Yellowstone

Thomas Moran's Grand Canyon of the Colorado.

None of the areas explored by the men who conducted the great surveys of the West in the years following the Civil War so captured the imagination of Americans as Yosemite and Yellowstone. Although most of the work of the surveys served to prepare the way for the settlement and economic exploitation of the West, the survey explorers of Yosemite, which is located on the western slope of the Sierra Nevada in north-central California, and of Yellowstone, which is in the northwest corner of Wyoming, found these regions to be so spectacularly beautiful that it was suggested almost immediately that they be preserved in their pristine state for the perpetual enjoyment of the American people. Thus, in 1864 Yosemite was made the first state park; eight years later, by act of Congress, Yellowstone became the first national park. The language of the Yellowstone legislation of 1872 expressed the philosophy behind these pioneering acts of conservation; the law was enacted for the "preservation from injury or spoilation of all timber, mineral deposits, natural curiosities or wonders within said park and their preservation in their natural condition."

The work of two great American painters affiliated with the surveys, Albert Bierstadt and Thomas Moran, was instrumental in bringing the wonders of these two regions before the American public and convincing Congress and the president to set these lands forever aside. Some of their work may be seen on these pages.

Moran's most famous version of the Grand Canyon of the Yellowstone. Although he declared the scene "beyond the reach of human art," Moran completed several different versions on this same motif. The original, completed in 1872, measured 7 feet by 12 feet and was immediately purchased by Congress to hang in the Capitol. Note the tiny human figures on the ledge in the foreground, included to give the viewer a sense of the immense scope of the vista the artist is portraying.

Moran's *Grand Canyon of the Yellowstone.*
Although the surveys are remembered for their
pioneering use of photography to document the
West, the paintings of Moran, who worked with
both the Hayden and the Powell surveys, were as
popular as the photographs of William Henry
Jackson, Jack Hillers, and Timothy O'Sullivan.

Moran's portrayal of Mammoth Hot Springs, in what is
now Yellowstone National Park; his good friend Jackson's
photographic portrayal of the same natural wonder can
be seen on page 94. Although Moran prided himself on
the realism of his paintings, they are notable more for
their artistic accuracy in capturing the effect of such
magnificent landscapes upon the viewer than for strict
verisimilitude.

HOT SPRING OF GARDINER'S RIVER, YELLOWSTONE

Albert Bierstadt's Bridal Veil Falls, Yosemite. *Although not usually regarded as a survey artist, Bierstadt accompanied Clarence King and his survey to remote regions of the Sierra Nevada in the autumn of 1872.*

Looking Down Yosemite Valley, California, 1865 *was savaged in its day by eastern critics, some of whom were simply unable to believe that such magnificent landscapes actually existed in nature. Although Bierstadt's painting is a romanticized depiction, his intent, as a more recent critic has put it, "was to capture the ideal sensation of the place . . . rather than to document it."*

Cho-looke, the Yosemite Fall *dates from Bierstadt's first visit to Yosemite, which took place in 1863. Bierstadt's work seems to perfectly complement these reflections on Yosemite penned at about the same time by Clarence King, then a young member of the California Geological Survey: "All stern sublimity, all geological terribleness, are veiled away behind magic curtains of cloud shadow and broken light."*

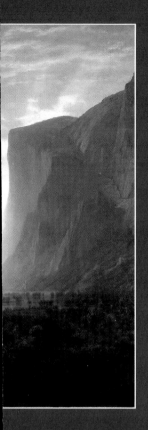

Bierstadt's *Cathedral Forest.* By 1872 and his time with
King, Bierstadt, like Moran, was being lionized for his
studies of the western lands. Together, his and Moran's
paintings seemed to support the popular notion that the West
was a special blessing bestowed upon the nation, a land of
scenic beauty and variety unmatched anywhere else in the world.

Bierstadt's Valley of the Yosemite. *"There is no phase of landscape in which [Americans] are not richer, more varied, and more interesting than any other in the world,"* Moran *wrote in the 1870s. Unlike so much of the West documented by the great surveys, the Yosemite and Yellowstone landscapes that inspired Bierstadt and Moran have survived, in no small part because of their work.*

(continued from page 64)

flimsy boats, becoming in the process the first white Americans to travel through the Grand Canyon. The lieutenant would have to make new plans.

Wheeler initially suggested another general survey of the West, but after discussions with Humphreys he refined his proposal to reflect his realization that civilian explorers now had the upper hand. He acknowledged that King, Powell, and Hayden had gotten there first, but he emphasized that his survey would be conducted for specifically military purposes. "The day of the pathfinder has sensibly ended," Wheeler would write in his annual report for 1871, indicating his awareness that the time when Western exploration was conducted for the purpose of discovery was all but over. Still, he saw many reasons why another survey should take the field.

King, Powell, and Hayden, Wheeler argued, were conducting what amounted to essentially geological surveys. While useful to a great many individuals, these were not of particular interest to the military. What the army needed was up-to-date, topographically accurate maps of the regions south of King's surveys—the rugged desert expanses of eastern Nevada and Arizona that were home to the

O'Sullivan took this photograph of a desolate mining camp somewhere in Nevada. The parched landscape gives the viewer a good idea of the kind of Great Basin terrain that Wheeler and King were surveying.

Paiute and Apache Indians. The location of potential coal deposits was not of the foremost importance to the army; what it needed were maps that illustrated the topography of the countryside it proposed to campaign in, charts that provided a "thorough knowledge of the conformation, the obstacles and resources of a country," according to Wheeler. The biggest job still confronting the army in the West was the pacification of the Indians, but Wheeler

pointed out that no officer sent to campaign against them could proceed confidently unless assured of a "thorough and free use of a full supply of topographical maps, upon which [were] delineated all the natural and economic or artificial features, and of the means of transit over the territory to be produced." The maps produced by the other surveys, Wheeler wrote, "were controlled by the theoretical considerations of the geologists." Wheeler proposed

An 1876 progress map of the U.S. Geological Surveys West of the One Hundredth Meridian. Although Wheeler's mapmaking and surveying were often criticized, he actually anticipated, as this chart demonstrates, the quadrant method that would eventually be adopted by the U.S. Geological Survey, into which his survey was consolidated in 1879.

to conduct his survey for the express purpose of creating maps designed for the specific use of the military.

Thus what would eventually be known as the United States Geographical Surveys West of the One Hundredth Meridian, under the overall direction of Lieutenant George M. Wheeler, were born. They represented, in the words of William H. Goetzmann, "an attempt by the Army to instill a professional spirit in its Western exploring activities to the point where it could regain scientific prestige in its own right, and with it control over all geographical activity in the Far West."

Initially, Wheeler's mission, as explained to him by Humphreys, was to explore "those portions of the United States territory lying south of the Central Pacific Railroad, embracing parts of Eastern Nevada and Arizona." Humphreys added that the "main object of this exploration will be to obtain topographical knowledge of the country traversed by your parties, and to prepare accurate maps of that section. . . . It is at the same time intended that you ascertain as far as practicable everything relating to the physical features of the country, the numbers, habits, and disposition of the Indians who may live in this section, the selection of such sites as may be of use for future military operations or occupation, and the facilities for making rail or common roads, to meet the wants of those who at some future period may occupy or traverse this part of our territory." His party was also to search for mineral resources and examine the region's flora and fauna. All this was to be accomplished in the summer of 1871; Wheeler was given authority to hire 10 scientific assistants and 20 general helpers—cooks, packers, mule skinners, etc. Perhaps the three most important members of the group were photographer Timothy O'Sullivan, the geologist Grove Karl Gilbert, and the journalist Frederick Loring, whose official expedition position was "barometric recorder and observer" but whom Wheeler was really counting on to write favorable articles about the survey.

Wheeler's fundamental method did not differ greatly from King's. From a central base camp, a number of scientific teams fanned out in all directions to carry on the painstaking work of taking surveying readings, while the geologists collected rock samples and the naturalists plant and animal specimens. In this way, a tremendous expanse of territory—72,250 square miles in 1871 alone, reaching from eastern California across southern and southwestern Nevada through southwestern Utah and northwestern, central, and southern Arizona—could be surveyed and mapped.

Although much of this land was still considered an Indian stronghold by the military, Indians rarely hindered Wheeler's work, and in many cases they assisted the survey as guides, hunters, or laborers. The greatest obstacle by far was the scorching heat, which averaged a searing 120° F. Surveying is a tedious and extremely exacting task under the best of circumstances; in these conditions, it became almost unbearable. By noon on many days, the men would be complaining of pain in their eyes from the merciless sunshine, and nightfall was hailed as a deliverance. Wheeler seems not always to have been an engaging or particularly attractive personality, but it is to his credit as a leader that throughout the years of his survey, under conditions almost always as equally challenging, there was very little dissension in the field.

In July, Wheeler's teams reassembled at Owens Lake in California in preparation for a survey of Death Valley, the murderous desert located between the Panamint and Amargosa mountain ranges near California's border with Nevada. Few men willingly entered this hellish region, which receives less than 2 inches of rain annually and where one of the highest ground temperatures—165 ° F— in history has been recorded. Wheeler's men, who attempted to cross this infernal expanse in two main parties, fared only a little better than most. Both groups managed to lose their guides but survived essentially unscathed, although several members, including Loring, the ever confident journalist, were felled by sunstroke. Even Wheeler, who in his reports seldom devoted space to the day-to-day travails of the survey, was moved to comment on the desert:

> The route lay for more than 39 miles in light, white drifting sand, which was traversed between 5 am and 6 pm, the center of the desert being reached about meridian. The stifling heat, great radiation, and constant glare from the sand were almost overpowering, and two of the command succumbed near nightfall, rendering it necessary to pack one man on the back of a mule to the first divide on the route, where a grass sward was reached at the end of a long sandy stretch, while the second, an old and tried mountaineer, became unconscious for more than an hour in nearly the same locality.

As one may infer from the passage above, Wheeler was a hard-driving commander who demanded a great deal of his men. On several occasions in Death Valley, by his own account, marches "extended from fifty to sixty or even eighty hours, with scarcely a single halt." No doubt it was this relentless drive that gave rise to a number of disturbing reports that appeared in California newspapers at about this time. According to the press, Wheeler and his men deliberately abandoned or even murdered the two missing guides, a topographer was abandoned and left for dead, a young boy was tortured on the supposition that he knew of the whereabouts of a runaway mule, and four Indians were tied to stakes in the middle of the desert and threatened with abandonment because they refused to sell the survey their mules at a reasonable price.

Historians have found these accounts difficult to assess. Richard A. Bartlett, who wrote the first comprehensive history of the Great Surveys, found the newspaper clippings cited above in an old scrapbook that he believes belonged to Wheeler, yet the lieutenant never mentioned any of the incidents, even to deny them, in his writings.

Wheeler and his party, including several Mojave Indians, depart Camp Mojave on September 15, 1871, for their journey up the Colorado River to the Grand Canyon. Strangely, in his report Wheeler wrote that he took only three boats, but this O'Sullivan photo clearly shows four.

There is evidence to suggest that one of the guides, a man named William Egan, later surfaced unharmed. Although it is unlikely that Wheeler or any of his men went so far as to murder anyone, it is possible that under the pressure of campaigning in Death Valley, where a missing pack animal or mount could mean the difference between life and death, and where the inability of a single member of the party to pull his weight could endanger the welfare of all the others, certain excesses occurred. Under such desperate conditions, one can easily understand why a commander might order his party to continue with their march rather than allow them to stop and search for a member who had gotten lost or had even possibly deserted. What is certain is that Wheeler did hold a great hatred for the

Indians, whom he regarded as less than human and often referred to as savages, barbarians, or assassins, and he was an outspoken critic of a government policy toward them that he regarded as so insufficently aggressive as to amount to peaceful coexistence.

Wheeler's next task was an upstream reconnaissance of the Colorado River, from his base station at Camp Mojave (present-day Needles, California) to Diamond Creek in

The Kanab Plateau, on the north wall of the Grand Canyon near the Toroweap Valley. This photograph was taken by William Bell, another member of the Wheeler party; the man on the precipice may be O'Sullivan, who took some of the first pictures of the Grand Canyon.

the Grand Canyon. As Powell was already in the midst of his second journey down the length of the river, and as in 1857 Lieutenant Joseph Christmas Ives of the topographical engineers had taken a steamboat far upriver, some have criticized this aspect of Wheeler's survey as a vainglorious and unneccessary adventure. The army wished to know if the Colorado was practically navigable even above the farthest point reached by Ives, however, and Wheeler proposed to take his three boats all the way to the Grand Canyon.

While teams commanded by Wheeler's most able subordinates, lieutenants D. W. Lockwood and D. A. Lyle, established supply stations along the river, at Camp Mojave Wheeler assembled a party of 32 men, including O'Sullivan, Loring, 14 Mojave Indians, and several soldiers and scientists. (With Lockwood and Lyle and then with Wheeler was the brilliant geologist Grove Karl Gilbert. Most historians credit Gilbert, rather than Wheeler, with applying the name Colorado Plateau to the lands on the north rim of the canyon.)

To use the word *sail* in conjunction with Wheeler's river expedition is extremely misleading. The Colorado's current is so strong that his vessels could seldom be sailed or even rowed; most often they were literally hauled upriver by means of a towrope carried by men walking along the riverside. This task is every bit as grueling as it sounds, and it was made no easier by the fact that for most of its length the Colorado flows between steep, stony canyons. A few feet of rocky shoreline exists at many points, but Wheeler's men were often forced to scramble as high as 100 feet up the canyon walls to find a spot from which to tow the boats. To make matters worse, the rapids of the Colorado are notoriously treacherous, and the boats frequently capsized; many supplies and most of Wheeler's scientific notes were lost in this fashion. Progress was therefore extremely slow; 15 miles in a day was spectacular, and at several points the expedition feared that it would be trapped in the canyons without food. It took the expedition 33 arduous days to travel the 200 miles to Diamond Creek, but, borne by the current, only 5 to return downriver to Camp Mojave.

Although Wheeler's Colorado River expedition was an undeniably courageous feat, it was of dubious scientific or strategic value. It proved only what Ives and Powell, not to mention numerous Indian tribes and the earlier Spanish visitors to the region, had already demonstrated—the Colorado, for the majority of its length, is not easily navigated. The difficulty of the terrain prevented Gilbert, the consummate scientist, from making many of his readings and measurements, and much of Wheeler's scientific work was washed away by the rapids. O'Sullivan was able to take some breathtakingly spectacular photographs, but the negatives for many of his most important pictures were lost en route to Washington.

The expedition also took its human cost: From Camp Mojave, Loring headed west via stagecoach, intending once he reached the coast to publish his accounts glorifying the bold men of the Wheeler survey. Near Wickenburg, Arizona, the stage was ambushed by Apache Indians and Loring was killed. His death inspired one of Wheeler's more blood-soaked passages. It resulted, he wrote, from

> the mistaken zeal, of the then peace-at-any-cost policy, that was for so long applied to the settlement of the Indian problem. Unfortunately, the bones of murdered citizens cannot rise to cry out and attest the atrocious murders of the far-spreading and wide-extending border lands of the Great West, and while the fate of the Indian is sealed, the interval during which their extermination as a race is consummated will doubtless be marked . . . with still more murderous ambuscades and massacres.

Wheeler himself would soon be in the fight of his life, but it would not be with the Indians. In many ways, the Death Valley and Colorado River expeditions of the

Members of the Wheeler party pose with their Mojave guides on the banks of the Colorado River in the Grand Canyon in the late summer of 1871. O'Sullivan, who believed the Mojaves to be "the finest specimens in all the West," may be the first seated figure on the left; that may be Wheeler next to him in the darker shirt.

Wheeler survey are apt metaphors for the whole—admirable for the energy and zeal with which they were pursued but ultimately marred by a certain superfluity of purpose. In the winter of 1871, Wheeler suggested a new, monumental scope for his survey. It was time, he wrote, "for a complete reconstruction of the engineer map of the Western Territories." What he now proposed to do was map the entire territory of the United States west of the 100th meridian, at a scale of one inch to four miles. The territory in question would be divided into 95 rectangular divisions, or quadrants. Somewhat later he would write regarding this proposal:

> The time has come to change the system of examination, from that idea of exploration which seems to attach itself to a linear search for great and special wonders, to a thorough survey that will build up from time to time, and fortify our knowledge of the structural relation of the whole.

Probably none of the heads of the other great surveys then in the field would have disagreed with Wheeler's statement, but they would have quarreled with the necessity of his carrying out his proposal. They suspected Wheeler, with some justification, of being as interested in

With this picture, taken in 1873, O'Sullivan became the first to photograph the interior of a Zuni pueblo. The photographer did not share Wheeler's animosity toward the Indians and on several occasions even served as a mediator at peace conferences in the Southwest.

building his own reputation and in restoring the army's preeminence in western exploration as he was in science, and they criticized his already completed surveying work, again with some degree of justification, as being in many cases unacceptably superficial and slipshod or simply useless for scientific purposes. (He failed to survey entire sections of regions to be mapped, for instance, labeling them as "inaccesible, or not immediately necessary to be known for military purposes.") Nothing that Wheeler proposed doing, their argument went, was not being done already, or could not be done better, by their surveys.

Wheeler did not help his case by his insistence, in the summers of 1872 and 1873, on devoting a great deal of his time, resources, manpower, and energies to the exploration of Colorado and the Colorado Plateau, a region where the greatest interests of Powell and Hayden also lay. In the summer of 1873 in Colorado, near the headwaters of the Arkansas River, some of Wheeler's surveyors nearly crossed paths with one of Hayden's survey teams, and a chagrined Congress was soon to learn that these two surveys, each funded with government monies, had set up their instruments on practically the same mountain peaks and were competing, for all intents and purposes, to survey the same land. Some might have found a delicious, ironic absurdity in the spectacle—in just a few short years the surveys had progressed from being the embodiment of the "first modern act of legislation," an example of an enlightened, rational, scientific use of government resources, to being representative of the excess and waste of an opulent and unrestrained era in American history known as the Gilded Age.

But at least one man was unamused. His name was Ferdinand Hayden, and he sent Wheeler an unmistakable message: "You can tell [him] that if he stirs a finger or attempts to interfere with me or my survey in any way I will utterly crush him. . . . I have enough congressional influence to do so and will bring it to bear."

Faith in the Grand Future

In Ferdinand Hayden, Wheeler had engaged a most formidable opponent. Hayden's survey, the United States Geological Survey of the Territories, was the biggest and best known of the four, in no small part because of his skill as a promoter of himself, his team's work, and the West itself. The congressional influence he boasted of was very real; none of the leaders of the great surveys was his equal in the use of photographs as timely gifts for influential congressmen and as propaganda to win public support. (He was fortunate in this regard to be blessed with the services of probably the greatest 19th-century photographer of the West, William Henry Jackson.) Although in his conflict with Wheeler he would style himself as the champion of civilian science, Hayden was the type of scientist that Congress could understand and appreciate: an unabashed enthusiast about the West who had no qualms about using his scientific talents to promote development and encourage settlement and tourism. According to William H. Goetzmann, Hayden believed that "to locate coal deposits, mineral veins, mines, timber stands, agricultural resources, grazing lands, water, irrigation sites, and tourist spas was . . . the duty of the territorial geologist. And, being no reformer, he worked with businessmen and politicians in indiscriminate fashion, always willing to help whoever was interested. His popularity was inevitable, and to his way of thinking it was honestly earned."

While members of the Hayden survey look on, Old Faithful, the world's most famous geyser, erupts. Although Ferdinand Hayden was not, as he sometimes claimed, solely responsible for Yellowstone being designated a national park, his survey did much to publicize the region's myriad natural wonders.

Another reason for Hayden's popularity was that as a scientist he was a popularizer; he believed that information about the West should be accessible to as wide an audience as possible, and the annual reports of his survey were prepared with this goal in mind. Goetzmann again explains: "He loved the West and its fantastic beauty, and being a self-made man, he regarded it as mandatory to share these marvels with the people." Such an approach meant that Hayden often rushed his work into print; the result was scientific work that was frequently disorganized, poorly thought out, and even inaccurate, for which he was roundly and justly criticized by his more scholarly colleagues. Yet no one could deny the achievements of his survey, which by the time of his clash with Wheeler—Congress would settle their dispute in 1874—were already considerable, and his advocacy of the West as a tourist's paradise, as well as ideally suited for permanent settlement, won him many supporters.

Ferdinand Vandeveer Hayden was born in Westfield, Massachusetts, on September 7, 1829, but soon thereafter, upon the death of his father and the remarriage of his mother, was sent to live with his uncle on a farm near Rochester, New York. From his youth, he was seen by others as absentminded, distracted, and impractical, hardly marked for success, but such outward characteristics are often the hallmark of the scholar or scientist, and Hayden was also independent and strong willed: At the age of 16 he refused his uncle's offer to adopt him and set out on his own to become a "professional man."

As was true for so many American youths of the day, Hayden's search for his place in the world took him ever westward. After teaching school for two years, he drifted, eventually winding up in Oberlin, Ohio, penniless but so persuasive in his desire to further his education that he was allowed to enroll at Oberlin College. Oberlin was a hotbed of abolitionist activity, but Hayden seems not to have been overly concerned with the slavery issue. Single-minded in the pursuit of his studies, he was an "enigma" to his fellow students, who regarded him, according to his future rival and colleague John Wesley Powell, as "an enthusiastic dreamer, who would never conquer in practical life."

Hayden's great interest was science, but in those days science as a professional discipline was largely the sphere of "gentlemen," meaning those with a personal income sufficient to pursue their avocation. Government sponsorship of science on a large scale did not yet exist, and academic positions were very difficult to obtain. (Their vindication of government sponsorship of scientific inquiry is in fact one of the most important legacies of the great surveys.) So on the advice of his Oberlin friend and instructor John Strong Newberry, himself a geologist and physician, Hayden decided to train as a medical doctor, in the hope that this profession would provide him the livelihood, and allow him the time, to continue his scientific pursuits. He completed his medical studies at the Albany Medical College in the state of New York and received his M.D. in 1853.

While at Albany, Hayden also studied paleontology and geology with James Hall, the foremost paleontologist of the day, with whom he shared living quarters. (Paleontology is the study of past geological periods through fossil remains.) Hall had earlier directed New York's state geological survey and was at the time hard at work on his massive, monumental *Paleontology of New York*, which would take him 47 years to complete. After his graduation Hayden was sent by Hall on his first geological expedition—a trip to the Dakota Badlands to gather fossil specimens. He found the experience so pleasant that he spent most of the next seven years in the West exploring the lands between the Missouri River and the Rocky Mountains. Much of this work was done in conjunction with the well-known paleontologist Fielding Bradford Meek, but Hayden also worked for Gouverneur Kemble Warren of the Railroad Surveys, and he shipped many of the fossils he found to Dr. Joseph Leidy at the University of Pennsylvania. Leidy, who was already famous for his work establishing the evolutionary development of the horse, was responsible for developing the science of vertebrate paleontology in the United States and with the aid of the specimens sent him by Hayden and others was able to show that in ancient epochs the evolutionary ancestors of species now found only on other continents—camels, rhinoceroses, and elephants, for example—had once roamed North America.

Through his work with Meek and Leidy, Hayden was thus forging a solid scientific reputation for himself. He and Meek were instrumental in developing a distinctly American—as opposed to European—system of terminology to be used for geological history, and Hayden produced a geological map of the upper Missouri and Yellowstone rivers region that was the best of its day. It was during this time that the Sioux of the upper Great Plains became accustomed to the sight of the solitary, slight, bearded white man roaming the prairies for hours and days on end, often stopping to chip methodically at the earth or some stone outcropping in search of, apparently, a fistful of rocks and gravel. They called him Man-Who-Picks-Up-Stones-Running, for Hayden seemed always to be scurrying about, fearful that he might miss something. A colleague who worked with him under Warren described him as "a man of rather small stature, talkative and companionable, well informed, and very energetic and eager in his work."

By 1860, Hayden was already thinking about organizing a government-sponsored geological survey that would "lay before the public such full, accurate and reliable information . . . as will bring from the older states the capital, skill, and resources necessary to develop the great natural resources of the country." He was particularly interested in a more detailed exploration of the Yellowstone region, but the Civil War made it necessary for him to postpone his plans. From 1862 to 1865 he served in the Union army as a surgeon, with a brevet rank of lieutenant colonel. His scientific reputation continued to grow, however; in 1863 he was awarded an honorary degree by the University of Rochester, and upon leaving the army at war's end he accepted an appointment as a professor of mineralogy and geology at the University of Pennsylvania.

But Hayden was destined to spend much more time in the field than in the classroom, and he was soon back in the Badlands of Dakota digging for fossils. He still desired to lead a government survey, however, and in 1867 he got his chance when he secured command of a federally funded survey of the new state of Nebraska. Hayden's

The U.S. Geological Survey of the Territories enjoys lunch in the field near Red Buttes, Wyoming, on August 24, 1870. The bearded Hayden is hatless, seated at the rear of the table, in dark coat and white shirt. Cyrus Thomas, promulgator of the rain-follows-the-plow theory, is the gentleman in dark coat and hat, with his legs crossed, seated at the right front of the table. William Henry Jackson is standing at farthest right.

survey was a comprehensive examination of the resources of the state, with particular attention paid to those that were likely to attract settlement. As William H. Goetzmann has pointed out, Hayden's first survey bore most of the characteristics of his later, more well known work:

> It was a county-by-county examination of the resources of Nebraska, supplemented by a broad range of technical geological observations. His interests ranged from the location of coal and limestone deposits to observations on the cultivation of farms and fruit trees. Almost anything that constituted an economic resource he highlighted in glowing terms calculated to please the local inhabitants.

As would be true of his later work, Hayden's zeal to promote the West led him to make scientifically dubious propositions. The most notorious, made first in connection with the Nebraska survey and reiterated later in his annual reports for the U.S. Geological Survey of the Territories, was his promulgation of the so-called rain-follows-the-plow theory. The greatest obstacle to promoting settlement in Nebraska, in particular, and anywhere else on the Great Plains, in general, was its aridity. The plains are seemingly endless, rolling, treeless grasslands; the average annual rainfall is less than 20 inches and decreases as one moves westward. As 20 inches of annual rainfall was considered the absolute minimum precipitation necessary for successful cultivation of crops, the plains in this regard did not seem promising to prospective farmers, especially those from the heavily wooded eastern United States, where thick stands of timber were traditionally regarded as an indication of a land's fertility. Indeed, the earliest American explorers of the Great Plains—Lieutenant Zebulon Pike in the first decade of the 19th century and Colonel Stephen Long in 1819–20—had characterized the region as the Great American Desert, and ever since, most emigrants had viewed the vast plains, the forbidding Rocky Mountains, and the truly desertlike regions of the Great Basin as areas to cross on their way to the more desirable western lands—fertile California and well-watered Oregon. It was only with the passage of the Homestead Act and the beginning of large-scale immigration from Scandinavia and central Europe that the plains began to be settled in great numbers.

The debate over whether the plains truly constituted an American desert was vociferously waged, and has continued to the present day, but obviously real-estate speculators, railroad barons, and town promoters had a vested interest in promoting only the positive aspects of what the plains had to offer. So the treelessness of the region was cited as an attraction; after all, the land would not have to be cleared before it could be planted, and the climate was so temperate, according to the more imaginative boosters, that one need not worry greatly about the scarcity of wood with which to construct houses and other buildings. The rain-follows-the-plow hypothesis, as promulgated by Hayden and others, most notably Dr. Cyrus Thomas, who worked for both Hayden and Powell, became a pet theory of western boosters: It held that through a combination of processes, the very act of breaking the soil and cultivating crops altered the climate in man's favor, inducing more precipitation. One can easily see the attractiveness of such a thesis for western promoters; the plains might be dry now, but once people began to arrive, the region would be transformed, from desert to garden. It was a myth and promise as old and enduring as the American frontier.

Hayden's boosterism, although sometimes questionable scientifically, was well designed to secure him further influence and his survey ever greater appropriations. In 1868, he was able to extend his survey west to the Rocky Mountains along the basic route laid by the Union Pacific Railroad; for 1869, his appropriation was doubled, and the jurisdiction for his survey—now officially titled the United States Geological Survey of the Territories—was transferred from the General Land Office to the Department of the Interior. That year, his party, which included Cyrus

The painter Thomas Moran gazes over Mammoth Hot Springs. The photograph is by his good friend William Henry Jackson. "I have always held that the grandest, most beautiful, or wonderful in nature, would, in capable hands, make the grandest, most beautiful or wonderful pictures," Moran wrote to Hayden in 1872. "All the above characteristics attach to the Yellowstone."

Thomas, the artist Henry Elliott, and James Stevenson, a slender Kentuckian who would serve as the survey's chief executive officer and Hayden's right-hand man in the field, explored the mountainous region along the Colorado–New Mexico border and as far south as Santa Fe. Hayden's report on his survey's doings that year proved so popular that all 8,000 copies were gone within 3 weeks. His technique in the field was the same as that of King and Wheeler; after drawing supplies from army fortresses and establishing a base camp, Hayden would send a number of small parties into the field for a detailed reconnaissance. In this way, he could cover an immense amount of territory each year. Always, he emphasized the positive aspects of the West. If a region was too mountainous and rugged for settlement, Hayden stressed its scenic beauty and produced Elliott's drawings to document his claims. Remote regions were painted as sportsmen's paradises; elsewhere, Hayden assiduously documented the stands of timber, farmland, and deposits of iron and coal that he found. Sometimes, he even anticipated the profits that the shrewd settler could expect, as in this overly optimistic 1868 observation on Colorado range land: "It is believed that sheep will yield an annual income of 90 percent; cattle 50 to 60 percent."

Thus, his survey continued to grow. In 1870, as the beneficiary of an even larger appropriation, Hayden expanded his team. Among the important new members were the photographer William Henry Jackson and the landscape painter Sanford Robinson Gifford. That summer's reconnaissance took the Hayden survey along the Colorado-Wyoming border into the Uinta Mountains, the Wind River range, and the Green River country. Jackson took the first of his classic photographs, which in all likelihood were the single greatest promotion of the West as a tourist's paradise, and Hayden issued the data he gathered in a massive 500-page annual report. This volume was more than 10 times the size of any of his previous publications, but such heft would come to be standard for Hayden as he rushed to publish his findings. This approach contrasted sharply with the more scientific ones of King and Powell, who took several years to shape their data into a coherent and structured overview, but Hayden believed it was important for himself and his scientists to get material into print as quickly as possible so as to impress Congress and potential patrons with the immediate significance of the survey's work. Hayden also had no qualms about allowing scientists whose work was not directly related to the survey to publish in the survey's annual report and the intermittent bulletins he took to producing so as to get his work before the public even faster.

This approach earned Hayden much justifiable criticism. Other scientists, including Powell, believed his methods to be unscholarly and slipshod, and much of Hayden's solid theoretical work was lost in the welter of miscellany that the annual reports included. But Hayden believed that in immediately disseminating information about the West to a broad audience, he was serving the larger, justified ends of the survey. He described his goals in the forward to the *Fourth Annual Report*, which covered the 1870 working year: "Never has my faith in the grand future that awaits the entire West been so strong as it is at the present time. . . . It is my earnest desire to devote the remainder of the working days of my life to the development of its scientific and material interests, until I shall see every Territory, which is now organized, a State in the Union."

It was a faith that Congress shared, at least for the present, and each year the Hayden survey grew in size. In July 1871, Hayden took his 34 men on muleback into the Yellowstone River country, where they chronicled its myriad wonders—bubbling hot springs, gushing geysers, and incomparable remnants of past volcanic activity. Hayden's men were not the first to explore this remote and mysterious region—they were disconcerted, in fact, upon their "discovery" of Mammoth Hot Springs, to find tourists placidly soaking in the steaming, multicolored waters—but the publicity their expedition garnered, largely through Jackson's photographs and the extremely popular paintings of Thomas Moran (see the picture essay *Yosemite and Yellowstone*), was instrumental in convincing President Ulysses S. Grant to designate Yellowstone the world's first national park.

By 1872, Hayden was sending dozens of men into the field, in several different teams. That year was the last he emphasized the exploration of the upper Missouri and Yellowstone rivers, which were, he believed, still too remote to be of immediate practical importance. Beginning in 1873, Hayden shifted his focus to the comprehensive exploration and mapping of Colorado. He explained his motives to Congress:

> There is probably no portion of our continent, at the present time, which promises to yield more useful results, both of a practical and scientific character. This region seems to be unoccupied at this time, as far as I am aware, by any other survey under the government, and the prospect of its rapid development within the next five years, by some of the most important railroads in the West, renders it very desirable that its resources be made known to the world at as early a date as possible.

The Colorado portion of the Hayden survey benefited greatly from the work of two new members of the survey team. His fieldwork with King completed, James Terry Gardner supervised the topographic work in Colorado and introduced a more systematic approach, reminiscent of King's and Whitney's, to the Colorado survey. The artist William H. Holmes was, in the opinion of William H. Goetzmann, "perhaps the greatest artist-topographer and

A mile below the Grand Canyon's rim, the Colorado River flows. A Jackson photograph.

man of many talents that the West ever produced." Chief among his gifts was an uncanny ability to reproduce in drawings the geological essence of the West's twisted and broken ridges, canyons, and mountains. The resulting drawings, which would illustrate Gardner's *Atlas of Colorado*, were masterpieces of both scientific observation and artistic creation, more valuable scientifically than most maps or photographs.

Jackson, a rugged campaigner who would lug his many pounds of photographic equipment just about anywhere, was present at both of the great discoveries of the Colorado years. (On less rugged terrain, an army ambulance carried 300 pounds of Jackson's equipment and also served as a rolling darkroom; for rougher going, the photographer relied on the sure feet and strong back of his fat little mule, Hypo.) In the summer of 1873, a team consisting of Jackson, Hayden, Holmes, Gardner, Josiah Dwight Whitney,

and several others "discovered," in the Sawatch Range of the Rockies in central Colorado, not far from the Eagle River, the Mount of the Holy Cross, a towering peak, over 13,000 feet high, whose summit was crowned with a great cross of snow. The mount had been the subject of legend and speculation for years, but its exact location had remained uncertain, and Jackson's photographs (along with a painting done by Moran, who visited it the next summer) caused a sensation. To many Americans, its existence seemed to confirm that God had indeed conferred a special blessing on their land. Although of little practical or scientific value, the discovery of the Mount of the Holy Cross was perhaps the Hayden survey's most well known achievement.

The following summer, Jackson was searching for photographic opportunities in the rugged San Juan Mountains of southwest Colorado, along the Mancos River. Along

The most famous image of the West produced by the Hayden survey was Jackson's Mountain of the Holy Cross. *The most popular attraction of the Centennial Exposition held in Philadelphia in 1876, it was regarded as a manifestation of divine approval of the American settlement of the West, "an outward sign," according to William H. Goetzmann, one of the foremost historians of the exploration of the West, "that God himself had blessed the westward course of empire."*

the steep canyons through which the Mancos flowed he discovered a number of remarkably well preserved cliff dwellings, the remnants of an Indian civilization that had flourished for centuries before the arrival of Columbus and other Europeans in North America. King, Powell,

Jackson's photograph of the sheer rock wall in Mancos Canyon where he discovered ruins of the cliff dwellings of the Anasazi. The ruins are about halfway up—800 feet—the face of the rock wall in a notch Jackson was able to reach "with the aid of an old dead tree and some ancient footholds." Like the pueblos of the Zuni and Hopi Indians, the houses of the Anasazi were multistoried dwellings with many interconnected rooms.

Wheeler, Hayden, and their scientists had made countless discoveries relating to America's geological past; here was splendid new evidence of its human history and testimony to the considerable cultural achievements of its native people. Jackson's photographs captured perfectly the haunting, magnificent beauty and ancient power of the ruins. In 1876 they were—along with models of the dwellings that he and Holmes constructed and his photographs and Moran's painting of the Mount of the Holy Cross—

John Moss (standing), an old prospector and guide who led Jackson to the Anasazi ruins in Mancos Canyon, and Ernest Ingersoll, a journalist affiliated with the Hayden survey, pose next to a cliff dwelling. The discovery of the ruins was "worth everything I possessed," said Jackson.

a popular draw at the Centennial Exhibition held in Philadelphia to celebrate the nation's 100th birthday.

By that time, Hayden was all too aware that his survey did not have Colorado to itself. He had in 1874, as promised, mustered all his considerable support to crush Wheeler after their dispute. There was "not a single square mile of the Rocky Mountain region sufficiently accurate and in detail on the [Wheeler] maps that we could use for scientific purposes," Hayden charged, and Powell agreed, characterizing much of Wheeler's work as useless. A number of prominent Yale scientists wrote Congress criticizing Wheeler; Gardner alleged that the lieutenant "had marched round and looked into but did not enter . . . great regions as large as Connecticut and Rhode Island together." Whitney, who believed that Hayden was "ignorant" but considered it his duty to support civilian science at the expense of the military, charged that Wheeler was pursuing a political and personal agenda rather than a scientific one and that his work was unneccessary. "Thus far the field-work of Wheeler's survey," Whitney wrote, "has been almost exclusively carried on in the same region in which Messrs. Powell and Gardner have been employed, and it is evident that this has not been done without design. It has been, and probably still is, the wish of the engineer bureau to put a stop to all topographical work done in the region west of the one hundredth meridian, except such as may be under their own direction."

Despite such damning testimony from such an impressive array of witnesses, Hayden did not win the crushing victory he had been so sure of. The president, Ulysses S. Grant, perhaps not surprisingly, backed the army, and Congress concluded that although both the Hayden and the Powell surveys were more accurate than Wheeler's, "there is an abundance of work for the best talents of both the War and Interior Departments in the scientific questions of the Western Territories for many years to come."

So Hayden's men returned to the field. Jackson and Holmes returned to the Mancos Canyon area to continue photographing and drawing the fascinating ruins there; Gardner and his team of topographers endured an Indian ambush, several forest fires and flash floods, and a dangerous lightning strike as they carried on with their mapping. But the Hayden survey's most significant work was behind it, and when Hayden clashed with John Wesley Powell in 1877 over whose survey should have primacy in Colorado, the days of the U.S. Geological Survey of the Territories were numbered.

Ferdinand Hayden on horseback. "A towering but typical figure of his time," according to Goetzmann, Hayden was "careless, wasteful of his talent, undisciplined, eclectic, indiscriminating, one part sham and much a showman" but "nonetheless a serious, able, and dedicated man."

Prophet of
the Arid Lands

John Wesley Powell was the most important of the leaders of the four surveys not simply because his two river journeys down the Colorado River constituted the single greatest feat of post–Civil War western exploration but because he possessed the most insightful and far-reaching scientific mind of the quartet. He combined King's skill as a theoretical geologist and his flair as an outdoorsman and a man of action with Wheeler's drive and ambition and Hayden's love of the West and dedication to its settlement, but Powell stood alone in the degree to which he questioned the already apparent pattern of settlement and economic development of the western lands. Powell was perhaps the only one of the four to fully realize that conflicts unresolved east of the Mississippi—how public land was to be distributed, the proper role of federal and local government in regulating settlement and development and allocating resources—were to be played out in the West, with potentially disastrous consequences. Like King, Wheeler, and Hayden, he harbored an immense appreciation for the uniqueness and beauty of the West, but he outdid them in the extent to which he recognized that the region's singularity demanded a new set of concepts and ideas to regulate its settlement. Powell also differed from the others in the immensity of his appreciation for the native peoples of the West and their culture and in his

John "Jack" Hillers, chief photographer for John Wesley Powell's U.S. Geological and Geographical Survey of the Rocky Mountains, took this photograph of the cascading High Falls in Bullion Canyon, Utah, in 1874. Hillers's photos of the Plateau Province are now considered classics.

devotion to understanding their past and present way of life so as to help them build a meaningful future.

Like his counterparts, Powell was by birth an easterner; like Hayden's, the course of his life from his earliest days flowed relentlessly westward; again like Hayden, he was an essentially self-educated and self-made man. He was born on March 24, 1834, in Mount Morris, a small village in upstate Livingston County, New York, about 35 miles southwest of Rochester. His father, Joseph Powell, was a circuit-riding Methodist preacher who also tended to a succession of small farms; he was also a staunch and outspoken abolitionist. In 1841, the family moved to Jackson, Ohio, another small town, some 25 miles southeast of Chillicothe.

Here Powell came under the sway of one of the most important formative influences of his life, George Crookham, an eccentric, self-styled educator who maintained in his home a personal museum of natural history and ethnological specimens. The elder Powell's vociferous abolitionism made him a figure of some controversy in the community, and because John Wesley was not hesitant in defending his father's position on slavery, he was often involved in fights at school. As a result, his father sent him to study with Crookham. With Crookham, young Powell read haphazardly in such classics as Edward Gibbon's *History of the Decline and Fall of the Roman Empire*, conducted a number of homemade scientific experiments, and, most important, spent hours outdoors on field trips, observing nature and its processes and collecting specimens. But Crookham, too, had managed to enrage public opinion, and one day a drunken mob torched his two-room log cabin, which was residence, school, laboratory, and museum, and the lessons ended.

The Powells loaded up a covered wagon and moved on, in 1846 to Walworth County, Wisconsin, several years later to Bonus Prairie, Illinois. Much of the hard work of maintaining the family farm fell on John Wesley and his two brothers and two sisters, leaving him little time for formal education, but he read whenever he could, whatever he could lay his hands on. In 1852 or thereabouts, he took a job as a teacher in a one-room schoolhouse in Jefferson County in southern Wisconsin, for which he was paid $14 a month. The job was a considerable challenge, for many of his students were older than he was, and Powell's learning, at first, was no greater than theirs, but he possessed a tremendous capacity for hard work and by dint of countless candlelight sessions in the stark room where he boarded had soon become proficient in geometry and the higher mathematics as well as a number of the sciences. His teaching methods owed much to Crookham, with a considerable emphasis placed on natural history and field trips into the wild.

For the rest of the decade, Powell pursued his quest for knowledge and experience with a restless intensity. He alternated teaching positions at a number of schools in Illinois and brief periods of attendance at a host of different colleges with long trips into the wilderness to satisfy his fascination with natural history and to collect specimens of plants, animals, shells, rocks, and fossils. In 1855 he tramped about Wisconsin for four months hunting specimens; the following year he traveled the length of the Mississippi River, from the Falls of St. Anthony in Minnesota to New Orleans in Louisiana, in a little skiff, stopping frequently for land excursions. The next spring he traveled the Ohio River by boat from Pittsburgh to St. Louis; in the fall he visited an untamed section of Missouri in search of fossils. By 1860, his reputation as a naturalist had grown so great—he had 6,000 plants in his private greenhouse—that he gave frequent lectures throughout the Midwest and the South and was elected secretary of the fledgling Illinois Natural Historical Society. That same year, he was named principal of the Hennepin County schools and fell in love with and proposed to his cousin, Emma Dean of Detroit.

Then came the great interruption in the lives of so many young men of the day, the outbreak of the War Between the States. Powell, an abolitionist who believed that slavery could only be eliminated by fighting, joined the 20th Illinois Volunteer Infantry. His leadership abilities soon convinced his fellow volunteers to elect him sergeant, and soon thereafter he was commissioned lieutenant. After procuring the standard treatises on military engineering and defensive fortifications and making himself expert on these subjects, Powell was named to Grant's staff and supervised the construction of breastworks at Cape Girardeau, Missouri. Following a short leave granted him to marry Emma Dean, he was made commander of his own artillery battery. In April 1862, on a battlefield near the Shiloh meetinghouse in southwestern Tennessee, Powell's battery made a stand in a hollow near a sunken peach orchard. The Battle of Shiloh was the bloodiest of the Civil War to that point; more Americans were killed or wounded in its two days than had been in the revolutionary war, the War of 1812, and the Mexican War combined. In the hollow near the peach orchard the gunfire was so intense that the area was dubbed the Hornet's Nest. Powell's men held firm, however, even when their commander went down with a bullet buried above his right elbow. The arm was amputated above the elbow several days later, but Powell went on to serve at Vicksburg and in a half-dozen other campaigns, ultimately attaining the rank of major.

After the war, Powell made his home in Wheaton, Illinois, and accepted professorships at Illinois Wesleyan University and Illinois State Normal University, but his considerable energies and persuasive and organizational skills were devoted to putting together an expedition to the Rocky Mountains. In the summers of 1867 and 1868, funded by a variety of organizations, including several railroads, the Smithsonian Institution, and various Illinois universities and scientific societies, Powell and a team of

His bushy beard and piercing stare gave Powell something of the air of an Old Testament prophet, and no explorer showed greater foresight regarding the settlement of the western lands.

volunteers that included his wife explored the Rocky Mountains. They collected a number of specimens of flora and fauna and scaled Longs Peak, which had never before been climbed. The feat won Powell much favorable publicity—a vacationing eastern journalist whom Powell met in Colorado described him as "well-educated and enthusiastic, resolute, a gallant leader"—but the most important result of the two expeditions was the determination it stimulated in Powell to explore by boat the length of the Grand, Green, and Colorado rivers, which collectively constitute the Colorado River system. In the process, he would undertake a geological investigation of the surrounding regions, particularly the spectacular, mysterious canyons through which they flowed. Various portions of the Colorado had already been explored, of course, but no one had done what Powell proposed to do: travel by boat from the headwaters of the Green River to its junction with the Colorado and continue downriver through the Grand Canyon all the way to Callville, a Mormon settlement near the confluence of the Colorado and the Virgin River.

Powell and his nine companions set out in four specially designed boats from Green River Station, Wyoming, a stop on the transcontinental railroad, on May 24, 1869. Three of the boats—dubbed the *Kitty Clyde's Sister*, the *Maid of the Canyon*, and the *No Name*—were 21 feet long, built of oak, with watertight compartments at either end. Powell's boat, the *Emma Dean*, was lighter, only 16 feet long, and built out of pine. In it, Powell would forge

E. O. Beaman took this photo of Desolation Canyon, Utah, in August 1871 during the Powell survey's second journey down the Green and Colorado rivers.

ahead of the others and communicate information about the river ahead by means of a complicated set of flag signals.

This first Colorado River expedition was not a government-sponsored survey, and funding came from a miscellany of sources, including several railroads and Powell's own pockets. Powell's team was similarly a hodgepodge of individuals of different backgrounds and interests. His brother Walter, a shell-shocked survivor of Confederate prison camps, was one; several others were hunters and outdoorsmen; a couple were former soldiers; one was an English gentleman looking for adventure; and another was a fugitive from justice in his home state of Missouri. None were scientists by training.

It took Powell and his men 100 days to complete their river journey. Its completion made the Major, as the bushy-bearded Powell was known to his men, a national hero, but there had been several points during the journey when his men feared for their safety. The *No Name* was wrecked by rocks and rapids in Lodore Canyon, and the *Maid of the Canyon* was almost lost in similar fashion. The Major remained imperturbable throughout. His men appreciated his confidence, but there were times when, trapped, as it seemed, between towering canyon walls and raging, seemingly unnavigable rapids ahead, their unappetizing supplies of rancid bacon and dried apples dwindling, they were exasperated by his insistence on dawdling to make scientific measurements and observations. "If he can only study geology he will be happy without food or shelter," one crew member wrote, "but the rest of us are not afflicted with it to [such] an alarming extent." For Powell's men, concerned first and foremost with survival, the desolate beauty of the canyons—"wherever we look there is but a wilderness of rocks, deep gorges where the rivers are lost below cliffs and towers and pinnacles and ten thousand strangely carved forms in every direction, and beyond them mountains blending with the clouds,"

Powell wrote—soon ceased to fascinate, the loneliness of these isolated regions grew overpowering, and Powell's excitement at finding one of the last undiscovered rivers—the Dirty Devil—and the last unknown mountain range—the Henry—in the United States was largely incomprehensible.

The crisis came on August 27. The party, by then deep into the Grand Canyon, had been halted by the most fearsome set of rapids they had yet encountered. Supplies were so low that starvation seemed a real possibility. Three of the men—Bill Dunn and the brothers Oramel and Seneca Howland—were convinced that the expedition could proceed no farther by water and proposed to hike up and out of the canyon over land. Powell disagreed; he believed that the rapids could be traversed, as had the others that had been encountered, by lowering the boats down and through them by means of towlines manipulated by the men from shore. He also argued, with more intuition than certainty, that this was the last dangerous stretch of water to be conquered, and he believed Callville to be less than 90 miles away—a quick jaunt with no rapids to hinder them. All but Dunn and the Howlands agreed with the Major; the next morning, after a breakfast "solemn as a funeral," the unconvinced trio went their own way.

After a couple of shaky moments, Powell and the remaining men succeeded in running the rapids; three days later they arrived in Callville. Their emergence from the canyons was reported with joy in the nation's newspapers, several of which had earlier reported their deaths. Their companions had not been so lucky, however; shortly after leaving the river party, the Howlands and Dunn had been ambushed and killed by Indians. Some subsequent reports by members of the expedition suggested that the Major had in fact forced the departure of Dunn, with whom he had had a series of disagreements, and that the Howlands had left him out of solidarity with their comrade. Powell's own version was that the separation had been the result of an honest disagreement over the proper course of action and that personal animosity did not come into play, but historians point out that Powell's published narrative of the expedition, the fascinating *Exploration of the Colorado River and Its Canyons*, unaccountably mixes episodes and elements of both his river journeys into what is ostensibly the story of the 1869 exploration and is thus a somewhat unreliable source. The matter remains open to dispute, but it seems unlikely, given what is known of Powell's character, that he would have deliberately marooned three men under such circumstances.

The journey strengthened Powell's fascination with what he termed the Plateau Province, the huge region of plateaus and mesas that stretches from the western slopes of Colorado to the eastern edge of the Great Basin and comprises all of eastern and southern Utah, part of western Colorado, and part of northern New Mexico and northern Arizona. It is, in the words of Powell's biographer Wallace Stegner, "scenically the most spectacular and humanly the least usable of our regions." Its unsuitability for significant human settlement would prove to be both a help and a hindrance to Powell as he secured, in the summer of 1870, the government appropriations creating the U.S. Geological and Geographical Survey of the Rocky Mountains and carried out his future explorations: For several years, Powell's survey remained smaller and not as well funded as the others, but the seeming lack of immediate practical usefulness of its work meant that the Major was allowed to work rather independently under the auspices of first the Smithsonian Institution and then the Department of the Interior. It meant as well that he could pay considerably less attention than his counterparts to locating mineral deposits, stands of timber, and other potential economic resources certain to delight congressmen and capitalists and devote more time to understanding the processes of nature that had created such a unique landscape.

Powell's second Green and Colorado rivers expedition

took place in the summer of 1871 and combined overland and river operations. None of the men from the first expedition went downriver again, but the experience Powell had gained on that journey helped ensure that the second would be less harrowing. Surprisingly, Powell again took no formally trained scientists with him, even though the expedition was to be the first phase of a comprehensive topographical and geological mapping of the Plateau Province. However, Powell's brother-in-law Almon H.

Thompson, though not formally trained, would in time
become a first-rate topographer, as would 17-year-old
Frederick Dellenbaugh, the expedition's artist. On-the-job
training became something of a hallmark of the Powell
survey: Jack Hillers, a German immigrant hired initially
as a teamster, would eventually become the survey's extremely accomplished photographer. Powell himself was
only intermittently present on the river, absenting himself
at intervals to tend to other tasks, such as the exploration

*Three Patriarchs in Zion
Canyon, Utah, which Hillers
photographed during Powell's
exploration of this region, along
the east fork of the Virgin River,
in 1872.*

of the majestic canyon-and-plateau region that would become Zion National Park. When present, he usually conducted operations from a desk chair lashed to the middle
deck of the *Emma Dean*, whence he would sometimes
declaim the words of Sir Walter Scott, Alfred Lord Ten-
nyson, or Henry Wadsworth Longfellow as the boats
coursed downriver.

Delegation of authority would become increasingly
characteristic of Powell's command as his expanding list
of intellectual pursuits and increased ambition for the survey demanded an ever greater portion of his time and
energies. Thompson, who had commanded on the Colorado when the Major was away, became the most important member of the survey in the field; to him belongs
most of the credit for the 1872 expedition that marked the
first exploration of the Escalante River, the nation's last
undiscovered river, and the Henry Range and for the mapping of the Grand Canyon, which was one of the survey's
most significant achievements. In 1873, Powell persuaded
Grove Karl Gilbert to leave the Wheeler survey for his
own, and a year later he offered a position to Captain
Clarence Dutton. To these men, two of the foremost geologists of the century, Powell gradually turned over the
geological fieldwork in the Plateau Province. The work of
Gilbert, with his meticulous scholarly approach, and Dutton, with his literary flair, complemented each other extremely well, and both drew upon Powell's theoretical
concepts. Powell was also fortunate, later on, to secure
the services of William H. Holmes, whose boldly rendered
drawings of the Plateau Province illustrated both Dutton's
and Gilbert's treatises.

Powell, meanwhile, was hardly idle. He occupied himself with his own geological writings, which are notable
for the clearness of his many descriptive passages, his profound understanding of geological processes, his emphasis
on the role of erosion in shaping the Plateau Province,
and his embrace of uniformitarianism. He also composed

A Paiute Indian boy, in traditional buckskin dress, poses for Hillers with Thomas Moran (center) and the journalist J. E. Colburn near the Mormon settlement at Kanab, Utah, in 1873. Although Moran won his greatest fame for his Yellowstone paintings with the Hayden expedition, he actually did a larger body of work as an illustrator for the Powell survey.

the articles for *Scribner's Monthly* magazine that would be collected and published as *The Exploration of the Colorado River and Its Canyons*. Although popular in its day as an exciting read, the book has been criticized for its looseness with facts—those who were with Powell on the first river expedition and remembered all too well his habit of downplaying potential dangers were particularly exasperated by his predilection, in print, for exaggerating the hazards faced; those who went with him on the second voyage were outraged that he mentioned none of them by name—but Powell was trying to write an adventure story for a wide audience, not a scientific treatise, and in his scholarly work was never guilty of such imprecision.

The Paiute chief Tau-Gu with Powell on the Kaibab Plateau, near the Grand Canyon, probably in 1873. The Paiutes called Powell Ka-pur-ats, which means One-Arm-Off. At the time he was engaged in investigating white injustices toward the native peoples of the Southwest, a subject on which he would deliver a number of scathing reports to Congress.

The Major had also become a sought-after lecturer. Perhaps as a result of his years as an educator, he was by all accounts a very effective public speaker, and he viewed his lecture opportunities as a chance not only to increase the public's understanding and appreciation of geology and the western lands but also to promote himself and his survey. In this he proved remarkably successful, and his personal influence and congressional outlay for his survey grew steadily. In 1874, during the contretemps between Hayden and Wheeler, Powell backed Hayden as the representative of civilian as opposed to military exploration, but by 1877 he had come to believe that the U.S. Geological Survey of the Territories was encroaching on his own turf. He proposed to Secretary of the Interior Carl Schurz that Hayden restrict himself to geological work while he, Powell, would concern himself with ethnological studies of the Indians, which had replaced geology as his great interest. Schurz ordered Hayden to comply, but the competition between and overlapping of the various surveys remained an affront to Powell's sense of order. Soon, he was pursuing a new, monumental agenda—the reorganization of the entire process and pattern of land distribution and settlement in the West and the consolidation of the surveys under one director.

Paiute Indians and Mormon settlers near the Virgin River in 1873. Powell is standing at far left; he had just been appointed commissioner of Indian affairs. Although Powell devoted much of the rest of his life to the study of Native American cultures, he believed the destruction of the traditional Indian ways of life to be inevitable, and he advocated the acculturation of the Indians through the teaching of English and other methods.

The End of the Frontier

Powell approached the question of western settlement from a different perspective than that of the other survey leaders. Both King and Hayden, by the implication and emphasis of their work, if not through outright advocacy, were essentially industrialists in their approach to western settlement—that is, they were greatly concerned with mining, mineral deposits, railroad lines, etc., and a significant portion of their work was intended for the benefit of powerful industrial and political interests.

As Powell saw it and outlined in his 1878 *Report on the Lands of the Arid Regions of the United States,* one of the most significant books to come out of the West, the important question regarding the future of the West was its agricultural development. The primary vehicle of western settlement, the Homestead Act, distributed public lands in the West to be farmed, and Powell believed that the ability of settlers to successfully work the western lands would be crucial in determining the future economic viability of the region. But as Powell viewed it, the Homestead Act, related legislation, and indeed the entire course of western settlement as it had developed after the Civil War ignored certain fundamental realities about the western lands. Decisions were being made based on assumptions that while once valid in the East, simply did not hold true beyond the Mississippi. The West, Powell argued in the 200 pages of his report, was so fundamentally different that new programs had to be implemented.

The Grand Canyon of the Yellowstone from the east bank, taken by William Henry Jackson in 1874. The four survey leaders recognized that the West as they knew it would be forever changed by the settlement they were working to bring about, but they firmly believed they were serving the idea of progress.

What made the West different from the rest of the nation, as could be gleaned from the title of Powell's report, was its dryness. Beyond the 100th meridian, with regional exceptions, the western lands annually received less than 20 inches of rainfall, the minimum needed for growing crops without irrigation. Many areas received significantly less precipitation. For most of its extent, at least as far as agriculture was concerned, the West did in fact constitute the Great American Desert. This was anathema to the West's promoters and boosters, but to Powell, with his unmatched knowledge of the region's geography, climate, topography, and geological history, it was bedrock, inarguable fact. Not that its aridity made it necessarily undesirable for settlement; indeed, Powell wrote, the soil in most places, especially when irrigated, was uncommonly fertile. But the reality of the West's aridity made absolutely necessary a well-conceived plan of land distribution.

Under the Homestead Act, homesteaders were granted 160 acres of public land. The land was distributed in rectangular tracts. This was a time-honored system of land distribution in the United States, suitable for the well-watered East, but Powell correctly foresaw that whoever controlled the significantly fewer available sources of water in the West would wield enormous power. Under existing law, whoever owned the banks of a stream could do whatever they wished with its water; an upstream landowner could use a watercourse's flow to irrigate his fields, leaving nothing for his downstream neighbor. In a land without rainfall, control of the available water thus became paramount. Powell also foresaw that in the West under the Homestead Act pattern of distributing regular, rectangular land parcels, it would be likely that one tract might contain water and thus be irrigable, while another would not. The first land would be valuable; the second, worthless. Given the prevailing pattern of graft in the distribution of public lands under the act—railroad companies, timber concerns, mining magnates, and real estate speculators seemed to end up with an inordinate percentage of the most desirable land—Powell anticipated even greater abuses, all at the expense of the small landowner.

Powell proposed that all the land in the West be surveyed for classification as mineral, coal, timber, pasturage, or irrigable lands. Irrigable land would then be distributed not in rectangular tracts but in irregular parcels conforming to the West's erratic, broken topography and the availability of water. Each tract would contain frontage on a watercourse and thus irrigable land, and these tracts would be 80 acres, not the 160 acres distributed under the Homestead Act. Powell recognized that in the West farming such a tract was backbreaking, endless work. Without irrigation 160 acres would not support a family, but with irrigation 80 acres would be almost too much to handle. Pasturage land would be divided and distributed in tracts of 2,560 acres—the greater size owing to the necessity of the immense acreage needed to graze animals—again delineated irregularly so as to guarantee that each tract contained water frontage and 20 acres of irrigable land.

A Timothy O'Sullivan photograph of the plateau country near the Colorado River. Powell believed that the West's unique topology and climate made necessary a new system of land distribution; the history of the West's development has proved the foresight of his assumptions regarding the central importance of water rights.

Because irrigation was so complicated and expensive, Powell advocated the political organization of the West into cooperative, locally governed irrigation districts. As he saw it, water in the West was too clearly a matter of essential public interest to be exploited inequitably as a private resource.

The release in April 1878 of *Report on the Lands of the Arid Regions of the United States* was an integral part of Powell's campaign to persuade Congress to consolidate the three active surveys into one. As he had put it as early as 1874, "Exploring expeditions [were] no longer needed for general purposes"; what was now needed, he argued before Congress in the spring of 1878, was a consolidated survey that would act as the most important government agency in a comprehensive program for the settlement and development of the West. He, Wheeler, and Hayden were invited to submit reports to Congress on their work. Hayden's and Wheeler's amounted to self-serving pleas for the continuance of their surveys, while Powell's was a characteristically sober and well-reasoned assessment of his own and his colleague's achievements, the areas where the surveys overlapped and had become superfluous, and the arguments for consolidation. (He was even gracious about Wheeler's accomplishments; since 1874 the lieutenant's mapmaking had improved considerably—Powell now believed that Wheeler's astronomical work "ranked with the best that has ever been done"—and his survey was responsible for 25 publications, 71 maps, including geological and topographical atlases and charts of the Comstock Lode and the Grand Canyon, and the collection of over 43,000 specimens for the Smithsonian Institution.)

Powell's argument carried the day. It convinced Congress to turn the matter over to the National Academy of Sciences for its recommendation, which was tantamount to a defeat for Wheeler, for the academy was a bastion of civilian science, opposed to the military's influence in the West, and for Hayden as well, for its membership, the leading university-trained scientific eminences of the day, regarded him as essentially an amateur and was scornful of the sloppiness of much of his work. In November 1878, the academy officially recommended the adoption of Powell's program of land-reform measures and advocated the consolidation of the three surveys into the United States Geological Survey.

The important question now became who was to head the new entity. Hayden desperately wanted the post, but so did King. In the years since the Fortieth Parallel Survey had left the field, King's reputation had continued to grow, augmented by the survey's many publications, including his own *Systematic Geology*, which used his findings in the field as a basis for a geological history of the Great Basin—a story that in King's hands, as one historian has put it, was "only a trifle less dramatic than Genesis." To King, along with Grove Karl Gilbert, who arrived at the same conclusion virtually simultaneously, belongs credit for the observation that much of the Great Basin was once the beds of giant prehistoric lakes. The survey, and King by extension, had also been distinguished by James Terry Gardner's *Atlas* of topographical and geological maps, an extremely handsome volume whose usefulness was only somewhat diminished by its hasty creation; and by Sereno Watson's *Botany*, immediately recognized as a classic and for many years the only reference book on the flora of the Great Basin.

And King was still the favorite of the eminences of American science, including Powell, who now stood in their ranks. Although he worked so hard for its creation, Powell did not particularly covet the post for himself, and he gave way in the face of King's express desire for the position. He had long admired King's work—when beginning his own labors in the West, he had believed the King survey to be the best run and had taken it as his model—and the two explorers had become personal acquaintances after meetings in Henry Adams's home and at the Cosmos

*Miners at work pause to allow
Jackson to take a photograph.
The four great western surveys
documented the location of
countless mineral deposits that
would contribute to the industrial
development of the West.*

Club, the Washington social organization devoted to scientific discussion and inquiry that Powell had founded. King was appointed the first director of the U.S. Geological Survey while Powell, whose land-reform measures were defeated in Congress—a combination of interests generally opposed the program as imposing too much government interference in the process of settlement, as too favorable to agriculture at the expense of mining and other industry, as promoting ranching at the expense of farming, and as injurious to the freedoms of the so-called yeoman farmer—contented himself with the directorship of another newly created agency, the National Bureau of Ethnology. The bureau was devoted to the scientific study of man—more specifically, under Powell's leadership, the study of Native American culture. Powell, whose interest in Indian culture dated to his sympathetic encounter in 1870 with the Shivwits Indians who had been responsible for the death of the Howlands and Dunn, would head the bureau until his death in 1902. When the most important of his work there, in particular his compendiums of Indian languages, was collected and published in five volumes as *Handbook*

of American Indians in 1907, it marked the most comprehensive examination to date of Native American culture.

But if King's star had continued to shine, it was with the fitful intensity of an orb that has begun to consume itself. Adams's best and brightest was destined to become the tragic embodiment of the dark side of the Gilded Age. Already, by the time of his appointment, he had become more interested in reaping a fortune as a mining entrepreneur than in further scientific achievement—his secret business ties with some of the members of the National Academy of Sciences had certainly not hurt his quest for the directorship of the U.S. Geological Survey—and he never devoted himself fully to his new position. Before resigning late in 1880, he absented himself frequently to scout out potential mining ventures and to hobnob in Europe. Ever witty and charming, he seemed increasingly the dilettante, interested more in socializing than science, playing on his reputation and connections for access to increasingly dubious business ventures, trading his name

Jackson at work near Buena Vista Peak in the Sierra Nevada. He is presumably preparing to document the arrival of a Central Pacific train; the advance of the speeding locomotive could serve as a metaphor for the onrush of American settlement in the West that the four surveys helped bring about.

for jobs as a consultant to various wheeler-dealers, end-lessly seeking the big score, and falling prey to unfath-omable (to his friends) personal compulsions. Despite the so-called genteel racism, characteristic of the day, that he often espoused, King in 1887 secretly married a black maid, Ada Todd. Although they maintained a clandestine residence in Brooklyn and had five children together, King managed to conceal his true identity from his wife until shortly before his death. In 1893, following a series of disastrous business reversals, he was hospitalized for in-sanity. His life afterward, until his lonely death in an Arizona boardinghouse in 1901 from tuberculosis, was a numbing succession of mental and physical collapses, fol-lowed by only partial recoveries. One of his last wishes was that Yale grant him an honorary degree at its bicen-tennial celebration in 1901, but the university, despite the intercession of the loyal Adams, refused.

By that time, King's successor as director, Powell, worn out from repeated, failed efforts to implement his land-reform programs and a grandiose plan for the topographical mapping of the entire nation, had himself been retired seven years from the position and was a year from his own end. Wheeler was dead, and Hayden, who had gone on after the consolidation to work as a government geologist with the U.S. Geological Survey, was 15 years in his grave. The last major battle of the Indian Wars had been fought at Wounded Knee, South Dakota, 11 years earlier; the buffalo was gone, the Comstock Lode was played out, and railroads crisscrossed the West. Four hundred thousand families had retained homesteads in the West under the Homestead Act; another 800,000 had tried to farm 160-acre tracts and had failed. Nine western territories had been admitted as states since the end of the Civil War. The process of settlement was far advanced, and the fron-tier was gone forever, eliminated, for better or worse, in large part because of the work of the four remarkable lead-ers of the great surveys.

A slain buffalo is skinned on the north Montana prairies in 1882. An estimated 60 million buffalo lived in North America when Europeans first began settling on the continent. Slaughtered relentlessly to clear a path for western civilization, by 1900 the buffalo numbered only 300 in the United States.

Clarence King, George Wheeler, Ferdinand Hayden, and John Wesley Powell were thus the last significant individual explorers of the American West. No doubt they would today lament some of the consequences of the West's continued development—the elimination of the magnificent, fearsome grizzly bear from its natural dominion, perhaps, or the acid rain and pollution that imperils Yosemite and other national parks, or, for Powell, the continuing tragedy of the American Indian—but all four believed that in working to facilitate the settlement of the western lands they were on the side of progress. And Powell, at least, would have been optimistic about the ability of science and government, working together, to apply their resources to solve these new problems. "The revelation of science is this," he said in 1882. "Every generation in life is a step in progress to a higher and fuller life; science has discovered hope."

The passing of the frontier: Jackson's classic North from Berthoud Pass. *The rifleman alone in the majestic Rockies is Harry Yount, formerly a mountain man, soon to become the first forest ranger in Yellowstone National Park.*

Further Reading

Adams, Henry. *The Education of Henry Adams*. Boston: Houghton Mifflin, 1962.

Bartlett, Richard. *Great Surveys of the American West*. Norman: University of Oklahoma Press, 1962.

Cooley, John R. *The Great Unknown: The Journals of the Historic First Expedition Down the Colorado River*. Flagstaff, AZ: Northland Press, 1988.

Darrah, William Culp. *Powell of the Colorado*. Princeton: Princeton University Press, 1951.

Dellenbaugh, Frederick S. *A Canyon Voyage: The Narrative of the Second Powell Expedition Down the Colorado from Wyoming, and the Explorations, in the Years 1871 & 1872*. Tucson: University of Arizona Press, 1984.

Goetzmann, William H. *Exploration and Empire: The Explorer and Scientist in the Winning of the American West*. New York: Norton, 1966.

———. *New Lands, New Men: America and the Second Great Age of Discovery*. New York: Viking Press, 1986.

Goetzmann, William H., and William N. Goetzmann. *The West of the Imagination*. New York: Norton, 1986.

King, Clarence. *Mountaineering in the Sierra Nevada*. 1874. Reprint. New York: Penguin Books, 1989.

Powell, John Wesley. *The Exploration of the Colorado River and Its Canyons*. 1895. Reprint. New York: Penguin Books, 1987.

Rusho, W. L. *Powell's Canyon Voyage*. Palmer Lake, CO: Filter Press, 1969.

Stegner, Wallace. *Beyond the Hundredth Meridian: John Wesley Powell and the Second Opening of the West.* Lincoln: University of Nebraska Press, 1982.

Stephens, Hal G., and E. M. Shoemaker. *In the Footsteps of John Wesley Powell: An Album of Comparative Photographs of the Green and Colorado Rivers.* Boulder, CO: Johnson Books, 1987.

Viola, Herman J. *Exploring the West.* Washington, D.C.: Smithsonian Books, 1987.

Wilkins, Thurman. *Clarence King.* New York: Macmillan, 1958.

Chronology

The entries in roman type refer directly to the four surveys of the American West; entries in italics refer to important historical and cultural events of the era.

1803–04	*The purchase of the Louisiana Territory extends American borders westward to the Rocky Mountains; Meriwether Lewis and William Clark begin their two-year expedition from St. Louis to the Pacific Coast*
1826	*Mountain men James Ohio Pattie and Ewing Young become the first white men to see the Grand Canyon*
1846–48	*The United States wins control of the present-day states of Arizona, California, Colorado, Nevada, New Mexico, and Utah*
1853	Congress authorizes Secretary of War Jefferson Davis to conduct a survey to determine the best route for a transcontinental railroad
1860–61	*Abraham Lincoln elected president of the United States; South Carolina secedes from the Union; Fort Sumter captured by Confederate forces; the Civil War begins*
1862	*Homestead Act passed*
1867	Clarence King is given command of the U.S. Geological Exploration of the Fortieth Parallel; makes first geodetic survey of the Great Basin; John Wesley Powell leads a geologic survey of the Rocky Mountains
1869	*Transcontinental railroad completed*; Powell undertakes a 100-day journey down the Colorado River, the first such journey executed by white men; Ferdinand Hayden leads the United States Geological Survey of the Territories; his survey reports become popular reading but are criticized as not being serious science
1870	Powell commands the U.S. Geological and Geographical Survey of the Rocky Mountains; the survey would concentrate on studying the processes of nature rather than furthering business interests; King, while climbing in the Sierra Nevada, discovers an active glacier

1871 Hayden leads a party of 34 men on muleback through the Yellowstone River country of the present-day states of Idaho and Montana; George Montague Wheeler is named to lead the U.S. Geographical Survey West of the 100th Meridian; his expedition would survey and map the desert expanses of eastern Nevada and Arizona, Death Valley, and the Colorado Plateau

1872 King exposes the Great Diamond Hoax; his *Mountaineering in the Sierra Nevada* is published

1873 Wheeler survey nearly crosses paths with Hayden, who vows to "utterly crush him"

1873–74 Hayden survey discovers Mount of the Holy Cross in the Sawatch range and Anasazi ruins in Mancos Canyon

1878 Powell issues *Report on the Lands of the Arid Regions of the United States*; the National Academy of Sciences advocates the consolidation of Wheeler, Hayden, and Powell surveys as the U.S. Geological Survey with Clarence King at the helm; Powell heads the National Bureau of Ethnology

1880 King resigns; Powell assumes control of the U.S. Geological Survey

1886 Hayden dies of locomotor ataxia in Philadelphia

1896 Utah attains statehood; eighth survey territory to do so

1901 King dies of tuberculosis in an Arizona boardinghouse

1902 Powell dies in Haven, Maine

Index

Picture Credits

Ann Gaines has a masters degree in American studies from the University of Texas at Austin and is the author of *Alexander von Humboldt, Colossus of Exploration* in this series.

William H. Goetzmann holds the Jack S. Blanton, Sr., Chair in History at the University of Texas at Austin, where he has taught for many years. The author of numerous works on American history and exploration, he won the 1967 Pulitzer and Parkman prizes for his *Exploration and Empire: The Role of the Explorer and Scientist in the Winning of the American West, 1800–1900*. With his son William N. Goetzmann, he coauthored *The West of the Imagination*, which received the Carr P. Collins Award in 1986 from the Texas Institute of Letters. His documentary television series of the same name received a blue ribbon in the history category at the American Film and Video Festival held in New York City in 1987. A recent work, *New Lands, New Men: America and the Second Great Age of Discovery*, was published in 1986 to much critical acclaim.

Michael Collins served as command module pilot on the *Apollo 11* space mission, which landed his colleagues Neil Armstrong and Buzz Aldrin on the moon. A graduate of the United States Military Academy, Collins was named an astronaut in 1963. In 1966 he piloted the *Gemini 10* mission, during which he became the third American to walk in space. The author of several books on space exploration, Collins was director of the Smithsonian Institution's National Air and Space Museum from 1971 to 1978 and is a recipient of the Presidential Medal of Freedom.